MW01164930

# Your Greatest
# Truth

**A Journey Uncovering the Great Secret of Life**

## DARIUS M. BARAZANDEH, ESQUIRE

Copyright © 2008 by DMB Real Estate Enterprises, Inc.

'Your Greatest Truth' is a trademark owned by Darius M. Barazandeh

All rights reserved. No portion of this book may be reproduced, stored in a retrieval system, or transmitted in any form or by any means – electronic, mechanical, photocopy, recording, or any other – except for brief quotations in printed reviews, without the prior permission of the author and publisher.

Published by DMB Real Estate Enterprises, Inc. 5050 Ambassador Way, Suite 210, Houston, Texas 77056

Please Visit Us At:
www.**YourUltimateWealth**.com
www.Your GreatestT ruth .com

Email: taxenterprises@yahoo.com
Phone: 713-961-1134

ISBN 978-1-4276-2207-5 paperback

---

&ampersand; **If 'Your Greatest Truth' has impacted you or someone you know in a positive manner, it would give me great joy to learn about it!** &ampersand;

**Please contact us at 713-961-1134 or email:**
**taxenterprises@yahoo.com**

---

Right Front Cover Photograph: All efforts were made to determine the photographer of this picture. If any information is known or obtained regarding this picture please contact us at: taxenterprises@yahoo.com or call 713-961-1134.

To those who have been, to those who will arrive today, and to those who will come after me: *Never Forget Your Truth!*

To my lovely wife Tricia who helped me immensely with her daily love and guidance as this book was compiled and beyond.

Special thanks to Troy Valos of the Norfolk Public Library's Sargeant Memorial Room.

# ADDITIONAL THANKS

I would also like to thank Dr. David R. Hawkins and Veritas Publishing for permission to quote *Power vs. Force* in the Author's Preface. If you would like more information about Dr. Hawkins please visit: www.veritaspub.com.

# Contents

# FOREWORD

Have you ever wondered why some people succeed, yet others continuously stumble with self-imposed limitations? Have you ever wanted something more from life; however, opportunities never seem to go your way? Have you ever been paralyzed to act but longed to be invigorated by the pursuit of your dreams? Do you remember a time when inspiration, creativity, and drive seemed effortless, yet now these feelings are momentary or distant? These are age old questions that have been asked by kings, philosophers, seers and great thinkers from time's earliest beginnings. These are universal truths that have eluded most of humankind for ages.

I have asked myself these questions throughout my training. I am convinced that this masterful book is not only life changing, but also revolutionary in its approach and clarity. It is a must read for anyone!

I realize some may resist embracing such clear and precise truths. My response is that sometimes living with the veil on is more comfortable than expanding awareness. I challenge you to read this story from the perspective that these truths are unquestionably real. Therefore, what does this mean for your own life and personal growth? I wholeheartedly believe that a more successful, rewarding, and invigorating life awaits you. Darius M. Barazandeh has opened the door. It is up to us to walk through this door and into a new life that breaks through barriers, transcends the ordinary and brings lasting fulfillment.

Robert D. Matzelle

Doctor of Psychology
Masters in Psychology

# 'Surprise' Is Not a Sufficient Word

Writing stories is not my traditional line of work. My last four books were legal-based investment programs, covering one area of my expertise: real estate and business law. I am by trade an attorney with a financial background. I hold a Juris Doctorate and a Master's Degree in Finance.

Nevertheless, from somewhere came this story. To tell you the truth, its messages arrived as many insights do: When I needed them the most. In early June of 2006, the flashes of these writings began. I was awake and working well past midnight. I began with only the intent to capture a few simple feelings and ideas, but nothing more.

Yet, from somewhere, a story kept entering my thoughts and my awareness. Although it sounds cliché, I soon found that the more I wrote, the more there was to tell. So, for the next 3 weeks, I put my business on hold, and worked energetically. I continued transcribing and capturing the flood of ideas as they came in. I penned quotes on napkins, the backs of envelopes and typed away at my computer. During all of this, I slept sporadically. In fact, many times when I tried to stop, for example to fall asleep, another detail in the timeline or a new explanation would be delivered to me. It soon became clear that these 'lessons' were developing into an amazing story. Timeless wisdom was connecting with new ideas and life-changing lessons. All of it seemed enveloped with profound insight, unique explanations and keen perceptions. Something was coming forward, but from where?

During one of these early writing periods in June, a few curious specifics kept coming up. A place with an active port district seemed woven into the lessons. Then the name 'Norfolk' entered my mind. Admittedly, I knew virtually nothing of the city of Norfolk; it was after all just a scribble in my notes.

As I wrote, street names and their proximities to landmarks also entered into the lessons. I was sure that these 'filler' street names would need to be replaced with factual ones. Since I kept imagining shipping and ports, I suspected that this 'Norfolk' would also need to be changed. My common mantra was, "I'll fix this later." I just kept going.

Six months later, January of 2007, marked the first time I ever viewed a map of the city of Norfolk. As my eyes glanced over the map I noticed some interesting features. I was happy to learn that Norfolk rested on the edge of a shoreline. The city also had what appeared to be some shipping activity. While these seemed like plausible coincidences, I also discovered that even some of the streets in my manuscript did in fact exist! The streets in the manuscript at the time were Main Street, Church Street, West Street and 34th Street.

There were more discoveries. For example, just as the story was written Main Street did, for the most part, run east to west. Also, as the story described, Main Street ran parallel to the water's edge, and as my writings had indicated, it was one to two blocks from the shoreline and shipping berths.

The proximities of Main Street and Church Street to certain landmarks were also identical to the story. Main Street ran right in front of a government building called the Federal Custom House. A large government building is exactly where I foresaw William, the main character, beginning his journey.

While these were fun discoveries, they were not earth-shattering and there were inconsistencies. I had included a West Street and a 34th Street in my writings. To my knowledge, these streets do not exist. Also, according to the modern map, while Church Street still exists, today it does not intersect Main Street near the waterfront as the story described. I also noticed that Main Street does not run east to west in a continual fashion, today it is diverted due to the construction of court buildings.

I realized however that my writings kept referring to 19th Century Norfolk not its 21st Century counterpart. I knew that since the time period of the story was the late 1800's, I should at least view a map from that period. After some research I discovered a 19th Century plat map of old Norfolk. As you can imagine, I poured over it intently.

Just as written, the old map revealed that Church Street did in fact intersect Main Street! At some point during the last 100 years, construction and development had overtaken this forgotten intersection.

Within moments, I also discovered that Main Street was, in 1885, a continuous east-to-west thoroughfare. It ran unobstructed from east to west, just as the wheels of a carriage might have traveled it. I also noticed on the old map that well before Church Street, a public structure referred to as 'market' was noted. Its outer edge was there on the map where my notes said it would be. Research told me that this area was known as Commercial Place, and it would have been one of the first landmarks that someone traveling east on Main Street from the Custom House would begin to see.

In the summer of 2007, I contacted Troy Valos of the Norfolk Public Library's Sergeant Memorial Room. I began asking questions of the old map and 19<sup>th</sup> Century Norfolk. Troy is a historian and has a deep knowledge of Norfolk's past. After a few emails we began speaking on the phone. Troy and I discussed late 1800's and early 1900's Norfolk. During our phone conversation, Troy commented that the eastern part of Main Street near the waterfront was made up of a 'red light' district complete with taverns and alehouses. Once again, this 'red light' district of old was in my writings and exactly where Troy said it would have been.

As you can imagine, all of this was quite interesting to me. Could I have known about the city's streets, landmarks and layout without traveling to Norfolk? Also, even if I decided to tour the city today, most of these particulars would be impossible to find. In modern times, there is no intersection at Church and Main. Today you cannot travel continuously down Main Street. Where the 19<sup>th</sup> century market once flourished, you would find a criminal and civil courts complex. Today there is no 'red light' district of old near Main and the waterfront. In fact, even the wharves which once were the center of Norfolk's shipping and commerce have long disappeared. Today one would find a waterside shopping mall bustling with tourists.

More questions arose. Could I have seen a modern map of the city at some point in my life and forgotten? It's unlikely and most of these features could not be found on a modern map anyway. How could my notes describe intersections that no longer existed? How could the location of Main Street, the old wharves and the government custom house actually be as my writings indicated? Could I have guessed that the custom house, Main Street, Church Street and the 19<sup>th</sup> Century wharves were all in close proximity? Could I have guessed the location of street names, intersections, shipping wharves, a market district, and a forgotten 'red light' district? Most interesting of all, the true east to west sequential order of all of these places mirrored my writings; all in a city that I had never visited and knew practically nothing about.

Other questions burned in my mind. While I have been a student of personal development for years, many of the explanations in these writings were quite unique to me. True, many of the insights encompass universal laws passed down through time, but many others I have never heard described by anyone, including myself. All of the information was interwoven with a deep clarity and insight that I just can't take credit for.

Even today, I do not have complete answers, but as I began to probe deeper I learned many things that mirrored the core truths of this story. For example, many have shown that we are connected to a higher source of insight and perhaps at some level to all wisdom. According to David R. Hawkins M.D., Ph.D., in his book *Power vs. Force*:

> *"The individual human mind is like a computer terminal connected to a giant database. The database is human consciousness itself, of which our own cognizance is merely an individual expression, but with its roots in the common consciousness of all mankind. This database is the realm of genius; because to be human is to participate in the database, everyone, by virtue of his birth, has access to genius. The database transcends time, space, and all limitations of individual consciousness."*

I concur with Dr. Hawkins and believe that many of us have allowed a higher source of awareness to teach or guide us at different times and to different degrees. A business person might simply explain it away by saying, "I knew it was a good deal deep down in my gut." Or, a concerned parent who learns of a bad accident involving their teenage son's friends might exclaim, "I just had a feeling that you should stay home...I am glad you did." As explained in this book, it is those who consistently connect with higher wisdom who are called insightful, perceptive, and maybe even brilliant.

The more I suspended my own limitations, the more I found that the lessons in this story were proving themselves real. And just as these writings foretell, for every question I found an answer (and there were many questions). For every trouble spot, test of faith or massive road block, multiple opportunities and insights came forward. While the book's core principles had been a part of my life for the last 18 years, they were leading me toward my own truth in new and exciting ways.

As the messages progressed, I came to realize that Norfolk's streets, intersections, and landmarks, and where they sat in relation to one another were not important. The streets and landmarks I had 'stumbled upon' were only signals; signals that at various moments, perhaps I was drawing upon knowledge outside of my day-to-day thinking and my ordinary awareness. As the purpose of the story was not historical perfection, places and names became superfluous. I decided to amend character names and take no part in trying to prove or disprove their veracity. All of this seemed secondary to my purpose and a potential diversion from what was truly important: The story's startling insights into the often hidden realities of our lives on earth.

Still, as this book grew closer to completion, I began to wonder how it might affect my current business. My legal clients and real estate customers were accustomed to my exciting penmanship concerning, *"Advantages of Business Taxations Under IRS Sub-Chapter S versus taxation Sub Chapter K"* or *"Updates from the Regular Session 78th Texas Legislature."* Many times throughout this journey, I considered putting the manuscript in a safe place and allowing a thick coat of dust to settle on it. How would clients and customers looking to master real estate transactions or to structure a business react as I delved into the great mysteries and secrets of life?

It has been a challenging journey, but I have come to realize that we must stand by our inspirations and our flashes of insight. We must live in the spirit of the higher self and the creative being in each of us. I recognized that by following my intuition to press on with this writing, it might impact lives beyond my own. For that reason, I knew that this story had to be written, its lessons presented to future generations, and its message spread to all who are ready to hear it.

I can't claim that this book is your absolute truth or even my absolute truth. No one can tell you what your truth is. That's because your greatest truth will always be found within you. As you read these writings, each idea or concept may resonate as accurate or inaccurate for you. In this way, you are being led back to your own inner knowing and to your own highest truth.

While I can't take credit for all of this, I do believe something very special lies in the pages of this book. I also know that it's not my wisdom, I only stepped aside and let it come forward and I believe that anyone else could have done the same. Echoes of a message delivered early in this writing still ring loudly in my thoughts. You see, "I am only a messenger of the great truth and it is a part of us all."

It is in the spirit of all that is good in each of us and the truth that connects us all, that I present *Your Greatest Truth*.

Darius M. Barazandeh
*Houston, Texas*
*July 2007*

# CHAPTER ONE

# You May Never Be the Same

I T IS NO ACCIDENT THAT YOU HOLD THIS STORY in your hands. Do not be afraid, but this book was created for you. If this seems too fantastic to accept, then brace yourself, because this story also contains your truth, your greatest truth. If you are not prepared to learn it, then you should set these pages aside now. Of course, this will be nearly impossible to do, since a part of you has always been searching for this truth. If you are ready to discover it, the hour is at hand.

My name is William Boyle, and while I will tell this story, I cannot take credit for the knowledge it will give you. You see, inside my story you may also find your own. I am only a messenger of the great truth and it is a part of us all.

This story will communicate to you the greatest and most powerful truth of humankind. Yet, for most people, this truth remains hidden unless the trials of life and persistence force its discovery. Sadly, most will live and die without ever learning it.

This truth was understood by the most amazing people of all recorded history. Likewise, this truth will be mastered and used by all successful, joyful, and content people of tomorrow. It has controlled your past, controls you at present and shall control your future. It is no exaggeration to say that, with this truth, you can change the world, but without it you may certainly be overtaken by the world.

Before your journey begins, I must provide two warnings.

First, you will discover two entities in your midst. Do not be fearful, because they have been with you since birth, and accompany you at all hours of the day and night. Indeed, these companions shall also remain with you for the rest of your life.

Second, you will unite with a part of yourself in the pages of this story. It is the same self which caused this book to be placed in your hands. It is the reason this moment is taking place right now. Do not be afraid, we have been patiently waiting for you.

# CHAPTER TWO

# Only Fools Would Desire More?

COME CLOSER, AND YOU WILL SEE AN ENDLESS line of roof tops forming a long procession of tenement houses. Though covered with snow, this icy blanket is no heavenly scene. The frost is filthy and blackened from the belch of factory smoke that encircles this district. The houses are so tightly fixed that in most times clean air and sunlight do not greet the inhabitants.

Come closer still and you will see a small window dimly lit by a flickering tallow candle. On the other side of the glass, a child's face peers out behind a frozen window pane. It is five o'clock in the morning on a frigid, wintry day in December. With prying icy claws, winter's cold has wrenched this child from his tiny bed. With an ache in his hollow belly, the child looks down at the dark streets below for his father.

His mother has not slept. She is awake at her chair, busily stitching with her needle. With loving eyes she looks upon her only child, and despite the cold air slashing about the room, her glance showers it with warmth. Perhaps this family shall have a trifle of coal by week's end. The year is 1862. I am four years old.

≈ ॐ

MY EARLY CHILDHOOD YEARS WERE SPENT IN AN area known as The Fourth Ward, on the East River waterfront of lower Manhattan. Livelihood depended primarily on my mother, at least until my father arrived from his business in the West. As I look back upon my earliest memories, I recall a dreary and uncompromising life in the Ward, Mother's diligent stitching and her untiring love. I do not recall ever meeting my father, yet Mother always assured me that one-day he would return.

My mother and I lived in a tenement house with four other families. Apart from her love, few comforts were found. Littered throughout our neighborhood were various slaughterhouses, soap factories, bone boilers and other industrial enterprises. The darkened outline of their smoke stacks and chimneys ominously stood over us. Like the watchful eyes of a foreman, one could not escape these omnipresent towers. Their shadows concealed the reach of sunlight and their vents spewed odors which crept into our living quarters. Their noxious fumes cloaked our lungs, shortened our breaths and caused many to become ill.

My mother worked as a sewing girl in those times. Today, one may liken her work to that of a seamstress. My first learning of numerals came from her labor. I learned of the number fifteen, before any other, as it was from here that our daily calculations began. As a rule, my mother was paid six cents per shirt, though she was required to furnish the thread. To maintain our housing, she had to craft fifteen shirts of perfect quality each week. The fashion house would not pay for inferior or unsatisfactory work. This stitching required at least twelve hours of Mother's time a day, every day. Such wages paid our monthly rent of $3.65. When I

*4*

was five years old, I learned that a pail of coal cost two shirts, and that bread and tea required three more shirts. I do not recall eating any meat or fowl in these years and I suspected such things would require two dozen shirts or more.

In the fall of 1868, my mother contracted an illness. Since my father did not return to help care for Mother, I was certain that his business was quite successful. Yet, I hoped that upon hearing of her grave condition he would come home. As her illness progressed, I navigated the city in search of anyone who could contact my father. A round, red-faced patron in a neighborhood saloon house admitted that he knew him. It was at this time that I learned more of my father's whereabouts.

"Oh Sir, you know of my father!" I replied beaming with delight at the discovery I had uncovered.

"May you please tell him that Mother is awful sick and he must return from his grand business in the West with due haste!"

With his jowls flapping about, the red-faced man laughed heartily. Then he stood up as to address everyone in the crowded saloon house. One of his stout hands tightly clasped the inside of his frayed and soiled vest, while the other flailed about as he spoke. Greasy faces of all sorts and shapes cast their murky stares at me; their expressions lingering in anticipation of the red-faced man's next utterance.

"The son of drunkard Boyle believes his dear 'ole father has grand business in the West, aye!" he clamored.

The entire mob laughed hungrily. One-by-one their faces lit up. Empty grey features suddenly blossomed with color and vibrancy. Lips parted, mouths gaped and it seemed that each was awaiting a succulent pig about to be served. As I realized the entanglement that faced me, my cheeks grew long and my stomach seemed to drop past the grubby wooden planks below. I looked away from the crowd and toward the ceiling and walls. Each was nearly black from years of neglect. I also became aware of the unpleasant smell around me. The air had an odor of rotting meat stewing in low grade liquor.

Once again, the red-faced man's loud voice echoed through the pungent air of the saloon and his words broke my blank gazes. With the skill of a grand orator, he delighted in proclaiming that my father would not be found in the great West, but elsewhere.

"This cannot be true, Sir," I murmured with watery eyes.

The round, red-faced man now pointed a plump, stubby finger toward the low dark ceiling. Addressing the hungry crowd, he returned sharply, "Grand business, my eye! Your father very well lies drunk or dead in the damp alleys of this city, right now!"

The stumpy, sausage-like finger that once pointed upward now rested firmly on my nose.

"Perhaps his fate will overtake you, as well; for you seem to be the same weak and feeble temperament as your father!" he commanded, with jowls fluttering. The ravenous crowd continued to hoot and cackle with laughter. One of the red-faced man's hook-like hands now clamped down upon my woolen coat and neck. When the grip of his claw was secure, he began to bellow and shake with laughter. Each shake transmitted itself through his grasp, and my body was thrown back and forth like an empty shirt on a windblown clothesline.

A rush of blood burned about my cheeks. My heart pounded so violently, I was convinced that it, too, wanted an escape from this dreadful situation.

Yet, from somewhere I heard a voice in my inner ear whisper, *"William, you can leave this place."*

6

Without delay, I marshaled all my strength, tore through the buttons on my heavy coat and ran from it. With my coat still caught in his snare, I escaped into the winter drizzle. All of my might was poured into my steps and I ran as fast as I could.

With my hands tightly holding my chest, I ran and ran for what seemed to be many miles. When I believed myself free from their words, I stopped and slowly made my way back to the tenement house. Although my tears had dried and my body felt entirely numb, the biting sting of the red-faced man's words and the crowd's mockery seemed to follow me, no matter where I traveled. They lingered around corners and in dark places. They found me at night when I dreamt, too. I dared not tell Mother about my experience, for her spirit and health suffered greatly in these days.

With little understanding of her condition and no means of support, Mother's sickness ran its course quickly. In late December 1868, she died. And so it was that the last pleasures of my world were snatched from my very grasp.

On the day of Mother's passing, I escaped from the throng of neighbors and social workers which crowded our room. I ran outside of the tenement building into the howling grey winds. The arctic air cut across my skin like one hundred icy knives. With skillful fingers, it overran every tear and split in my tattered clothes and, like iced hooks, it tore at my skin. Fortunately, I quickly learned from street dwellers that burlap sacks and abandoned newssheets could provide me with a modicum of warmth. Although winter's cold and a lack of food accompanied me at most times, I still vowed never to live in the dank and stale air of the tenement houses again.

One month later, I was brought to an almshouse for children. Today, one might call this place an orphan home or child shelter. This loving place was the Howard Mission on New Bowery Street. I was to remain there until a 'suitable' dwelling for me could be found.

At the Howard Mission, I was given an abundance of victuals and some schooling. Yet, after less than three months at the mission, I fled. I shall say that, in those months, a strange phenomenon arose in my thought habits. I began to suspect that a full stomach, hot meals and warm bed were 'apparatus of the rich' and should be avoided. Strangely, such thoughts did not arise from any dishonesty or wrongdoing at the home.

Since the reader may wonder why, as a mere child, I would run from such charity and care, I shall explain. My departure was set in motion by a seed planted in my mind. This seed grew and later produced a fruit. You see, before Mother's death, I decided that I must know more about my father. Several weeks prior to her passing, I began to ask many questions of Mother. No matter how she tried to favor him, my father's words were clear. Tears welled in her eyes as she told of his curses upon her: "You will be lucky in these times to toil among the magnitude of sewing girls of the city," he would bark. Mother swallowed hard and then continued to utter his warnings with careful precision: "Employers shall cheat, so take your trifling wage, since the world has determined your merit and only the fools will desire more." I learned that he believed wealth came only to those who cheated others. If wealth was found, be careful as "wickedness and wealth are close associates," he would charge.

With foggy eyes and a yellowed expression, she looked at me and whispered, "Son, I took to heart his belief of these things as true." Mother then grasped my hand firmly and said, "Perhaps it is true, William. Maybe people like us are ill designed for opportunity in this world. If you put your hopes into one thing, then the world seems to take it away," she warned.

As a young child, these words seemed to enter my very core with no obstruction. At such time, I could never have reasoned that they might control my consciousness. Yet, her words seemed to be more than simple warnings, but a path or destiny which appeared inescapable to me. "Who could know more about me than Mother," I reasoned to myself. I can say now that these warnings led me to distrust the Howard Mission and to leave New Bowery Street.

With no one to care for me, I wandered the streets and rail yards of New York's lower west side. I soon found a place among homeless vagrants and ruffians, most of whom were my senior. The children in this group were known as "gutter snipes," a term which, at the time, amused me.

From ages 10 to 15, I lived among these homeless children and men of the rail yards. All of them were born of similar circumstances as myself. As Mother warned, people of this 'sort' seemed ill equipped for life and advancement. Like clockwork, the world seemed to determine their order and rank. And soon they were all but forgotten. With little understanding of themselves, and not so much as a fight, they lived and died as millions of others before them: accepting whatever life offered and little more. In an orderly procession on each muddy corner, forgotten alley, or cramped stoop, they clutched and groveled for any meager handout or the discarded morsel that luck or charity might bring to them.

Without hesitation, I accepted these thoughts and patterns as a way of life. Their actions, attitudes and beliefs became my own. I reasoned that since the world has also determined my worth, I should accept this status, without fight. "Only fools would desire more," I thought.

# CHAPTER THREE
# Do You Know True Desire?

ONE FOGGY MORNING IN APRIL 1873, I AWOKE well before dawn. A heavy soup-like vapor covered the rail yard. While the others in my group slept, I had an uncommon desire to walk. Perhaps the fog's hazy veil played tricks on me, but on that morning everything was surreal. It seemed the rest of mankind and its trappings no longer existed.

It was on this quiet morning that an incredible thought was born. I began to think about leaving the city. I cannot recall how this idea came into my mind, but I can remember that, from somewhere, a change in my thought habits took place. Looking back, I can say that, as a young child, I always accepted the reality around me. I believe this was because I knew of nothing else. However, on this morning, something changed. You might say that, for the first time, my thoughts were completely my own and came from choice, not the words, moods, or acts of others. Current conditions ceased their hold on my body, and thoughts were formed according to what I wanted to see take place.

I must say that my idea to leave the city became similar to a special gift. I also considered it a secret gift which I kept protected from the outside world. As such, I dared not explain it to others in my clan. Although it may seem strange to you, the more I presented this gift to my mind, the greater my affection and excitement for it became. Soon, this idea filled most of my waking moments.

It was shortly thereafter that I happened upon an amazing discovery. I found that when I focused my thoughts on leaving by railcar, my mind brought with it images and associated feelings. I would sit and watch the railcars leaving the station house and see myself staring down from their lofty windows. I could feel the rhythmic motion of the rail car stirring my body and imagined miles of open track beckoning before me. The reality of moving beyond the dismal rail yards and alleys became clear and dominating. I felt an urge for freedom and a hunger to expand beyond my present situation. These things brought me so much joy that soon this idea ignited beyond a mere wish.

Although Mother warned me about putting my whole heart into something, I ignored this advice. And soon this simple thought grew to an overwhelming desire. It occupied my waking and sleeping hours without end. Where previously my life was centered on hopelessness, a desire for change burned within me. My true purpose became making this vision a reality.

I presented to my mind a single question, "How can I leave New York by railcar?" Soon I discovered that when I concentrated on this subject, answers would slowly come forward and soon my mind was flooded with possibilities. Immediately, I realized that random chance and begging had no place for me. As I could not guarantee the charity of others, I must ensure that I would receive wages or payment.

Another astounding realization seemed to come into my mind, as well:  I must depart from the band of vagrants I had been associating with.  Despite their pleading and dispiriting cries, I split from this group.  I must confess that, as a homeless young man, such a decision might cause me some risk.  Indeed I was scared, but instead of focusing on my fears, I lived in my desires.  When fear seemed to overtake my desire, I fought back with action.

I made myself available to merchants, rail men, butchers, soap makers, and others engaged in trade.  No job was too difficult or too repugnant for me.  For the butcher, I wheeled decaying animal carcasses to the debris heap.  For the soap maker, I cleaned out his neglected barrels.  Much of this required me to stomach the pungent and nauseating odor of decomposing animal flesh and fat.  The stench blurred my eyes, stole my breath and soured my mouth, yet it did not matter.  Indeed, many of these putrid smells were painful reminders of my childhood days among rancid odors of the tenement buildings, yet I continued.

In retrospect, I can say that, from my desire to leave the city, a purpose was born in my heart.  This purpose drove me forward.  Although I was surrounded by fetid smells, sweltering heat and backbreaking work, I discovered meaning and deep joy for the first time in my life.  One might say that, since this purpose created contentment from within, my external reality seemed temporary, fleeting and, in its own, way incredibly beautiful.

I would leave New York by way of the Washington Railcar Line and travel to Norfolk, Virginia.  I did not know of Norfolk firsthand, but had seen an artist's rendering of the city at sunrise.

The golden glow of the drawing could not be erased; it glistened in my mind.

Week after week, I re-doubled my efforts and made myself available to all shop owners and tradesmen. I gave my full and absolute energies to this purpose. When exhaustion and shortage seemed imminent, from somewhere within and around me, more energy and opportunity came forward. Those whom I helped responded in kind with wages, small quantities of food and minor provisions. In preparation for my journey, a storekeeper even offered me a secondhand pair of shoes. The butcher paid me a bonus that included a linen shirt and heavy pants! Before long, I not only possessed enough money for my ticket, but a fresh change of clothes. Even though I had no currency for food, I hastily bade a gracious farewell to my employers and began upon my journey.

On a bright morning in July of 1873, I walked up to the stately ticket counter and purchased my voucher. Joy of an overwhelming and exuberant nature built up inside me as I handed the clerk my fare. He returned to me an elegant maroon ticket. The top of the ticket had exquisite writing and the paper itself was so substantial. Never in my life had I felt paper of such a heavy grade! When my fingers clutched the ticket, my insides welled with an indescribable joy.

As my feet climbed the stepladder to the car, it felt as if the soles of my shoes were one hundred feet above the ground, quite figuratively walking on air.

CHAPTER FOUR

# Would You Have Listened?

AS I HAD ONLY MONEY FOR TRAVEL FARE, I ATE very little during my journey. The few crusts of bread and dried meat that I carried with me were gone quickly. I also slept very little, although I cannot recall the reason for my lack of sleep. I suspect it was the fear that I might mysteriously awaken, only to discover myself once again in the Ward or rail yards. Nevertheless, by train, horse and wagon, and then by foot, I continued toward Norfolk. Regardless of my hunger and occasional hardship, I had never experienced such elation and fulfillment.

I reached Norfolk, Virginia early one morning in August 1873. I arrived with a hunger so severe I was certain that my very insides had collapsed. My body was also very tired and stiff. From my time on foot, my feet were blistered and sore. I was not more than two breaths from sitting down, when something magnificent caught my eye.

A splendid sunrise began to cast its golden glow throughout the city. The thick radiating beams poured down from the sky with a mix of orange and gold brilliance. Around me, I saw the business of the day begin, and the sparkling image I clutched at the train depot was now unfolding before my eyes.

Sunlight energized the sleeping air as it flowed like molten gold through newly opened store windows and down cold dark crevices. It illuminated all the creatures below in an age-old dance of life. Perhaps I, too, felt an illumination, because my pain and hunger now seemed trite and unimportant. I felt an intuition to travel south to the water's edge. I quickly sought directions and started moving. At some points, I stepped at a quick trot, while at other times I ran. Although I could not understand the reason, I had a swift purpose in my stride and boldness in my motion.

With little rest, throbbing feet and the incessant burnings of hunger, another young man might have been preoccupied with rest and sustenance. Nevertheless, I had an impulse to arrive at the wharves and the water's edge. As to what I would do when I arrived, I had no answer. I only knew that I must proceed without delay, so I ignored all physical discomfort. With each step, my passion and excitement grew to such a degree that I began to fear that if they multiplied any further, the next stride might cause me to burst!

I sped through the many streets and alleyways of the city. I ducked under fire escapes, scuttled down lonely passages and ran along the bustling thoroughfares. I lost direction in brief moments, but kept going. Oh, how my body and heart raced along those streets that day! Although I tried not to call attention to myself, people began to notice my haste. First, a smiling old man pushing a small wooden cart somewhere near Charlotte Street cried out, "Who chases you boy?" Near the corner of Freemason and Catherine Street, a high-browed lady with a bonnet on head and a basket in hand noticed me. She paused from her morning errands to deliver her edition of the whole affair, "The poor child is unquestionably rabid! Let the rapscallion pass!" Just then, a short-framed man with an affable grin and a hat nearly equal to his stature, vigorously yelled, "Keep running boy! Don't listen, Godspeed!" All manner of warnings, proclamations and questions were hurled at me as I ran. It all made no difference because nothing could halt my steps.

Indeed, it may make little sense to you the reader, but a part of me knew where I was going, although I had no idea where my steps would lead me.

As I came closer to the wharves along the Elizabeth River, its fresh air and bustling activity mesmerized me. I felt such vigor, such life, and such liberty. I spotted three men unloading a small craft in one of the more moderate berths. One man was in the vessel passing cargo to two men standing on the docks. Immediately, I climbed aboard the docked vessel and began passing feed bags, cargo boxes and barrels to the men above. Not a question was asked of me, so I continued to unload the vessel.

I moved with great speed and gave every ounce of strength and concentration to my service that day. When my tasks were completed, I assisted others with their duties. I cannot say why I felt compelled to serve, but I found that the more I contributed, the higher my spirits did rise. Something was moving me, but I could not identify its source. Amazingly, it was that very day the berth manager offered me employment. I was also given permission to sleep in a small storage shed located in an alleyway behind the offices.

As I was the youngest on the crew, I seldom had the luxury of using loaders to move the cargo. Typically, I would move the cargo using my back; at such time, I was quite sturdy. In these days, I cannot recall a shred of thought dedicated to what I lacked. I only made full use of the resources I possessed. You see, the difficult labor did not matter, as my spirit longed for challenge and I felt unlimited possibilities within my grasp. The fresh ample air of the wharves, the cawing of the sea birds and the honest work I performed were a heavenly delight to me.

At some point, a cotton merchant and developer caught sight of my work. As he stood at his office window above the shipping berths, he must have witnessed my enthusiasm. I later learned that he told one of his assistants, "This young man brings back memories of my beginnings in life." He then said, "Summon him here today, as I want to speak with him."

Imagine my surprise when, on one morning in December, a formally-dressed gentleman approached me as I labored. He said that at noon I should travel to the large square building which overlooked the wharves. Of course, I followed his request and was soon led up to a room that was so large, I suspected that as many as 20 people must, indeed, work in such a place. As I remembered them, many of the sewing rooms where Mother had worked were far smaller in size and were occupied by as many as 30 women. From my vantage point, an enormous dark wood monument greeted me. It sat majestically in the center of the room and was adorned with splendid carvings and gold-colored moldings. I suspected that perhaps all 20 people might labor at this station, yet I saw no tools, stitching machines or any devices. I also found it odd that I saw no workers; however, I was certain that, at any moment, they would arrive. As soon as these thoughts floated into my mind, I saw a figure stir in the background. It was an older man standing by a tall window to the rear of this room. The man was dressed nicely, but not over-stuffed. He slowly walked toward the giant monument, carefully arranged a high-backed, leather chair, and then took a seat. Once behind this giant wooden edifice, this man's persona made it look inadequate. I then realized that what appeared to be a monument was, in fact, his desk! Immediately I wondered if a mistake had been made.

"Sir, please do pardon my audacity, but perhaps your assistant has mistaken me for another," I informed him.

"My boy, it is no accident, no mistake. You are here from your own doing, of this I am quite sure."

I wondered what he meant by these words, but I had little time to contemplate them. He asked me many questions and it seemed odd that a man of his caliper could take an interest in one such as me. He asked of my days in Norfolk and my background. We spoke for a time and I disclosed my upbringing in the cramped houses of the Fourth Ward, New York.

"Sir, I saw my mother pass away from the polluted eating and infected living conditions of the tenement houses," I stated blankly. "I was merely a child, but it did develop hopelessness in me. Then, sir, when the anger and disgust of my condition became so great, I had to leave all memories of that place."

It was upon uttering those words that I realized my path to Norfolk was fueled by my dislike of the damp, suffocating, foul air in which I was raised.

He asked what I sought to do with my life. I then responded in a manner that even astounded me. I spoke words that had never entered my active thoughts, yet I mouthed them with certainty and conviction,

"Sir, I have a keen interest in, one day, building decent and honest housing." I do recall a feeling of absolute shock at the words I had uttered. For the first time, I realized that my experiences of sadness and pain planted a desire in my heart. Somehow, my misfortunes were yielding way to a greater direction and a greater purpose.

The man was Franklin W. Wells, one of the wealthiest men in Virginia. He was a cotton broker, and owned a construction business and a cotton farming operation. He also was a majority shareholder in several lumber mills. In addition, his reach extended to land interests, as he held quantities of acreage around the city. His fortune was not passed down by inheritance, but was created by a unity of his mind and his hands. Mr. Wells, perhaps, recognized a part of himself in me. Hence, it was his belief that I should be taught a trade.

Mr. Wells instructed that, if I so desired, he would allow me to work in several of his businesses for a time. If I proved my worth after a provisional term of employment, he would then retain me for permanent work. I was to work for one year in his construction business, then later begin work in the lumber mills. I accepted this opportunity with great joy.

I savored my work and felt that this path would lead me to great things. Into this work I poured my will and spirit, and so it was that I excelled quickly. While I rarely spoke to Mr. Wells after that brief introduction, I was eager to learn more about him and his path to success. I asked questions and sought knowledge about him, his traits and his life. I imagined myself keeping pace with his accomplishments, and my achievements someday equaling his own. Within six years, I became a manager with responsibility over the Wells Lumber Mill No. 2 on the Elizabeth River. I was also given secondary accountability over several construction interests along the river. The year was 1880.

While I wished to work with Mr. Wells directly, it was not to be. Shortly after my promotion, Mr. Wells was struck with a condition of the nerves and muscles. His health and function progressively deteriorated. It was soon after my promotion to manager that he died. Nevertheless, I remained intensely focused on following his path.

# CHAPTER FIVE
# What Would You Have Felt?

M R. WELLS DIED IN OCTOBER OF 1880. FROM THE moment of his passing, I began to wonder if my background made me unsuitable as a manager. You see, it was the children and relatives of Mr. Wells who traditionally managed each of his ventures and held majority stock interests. With no connection to the Well's pedigree, and Wells himself no longer alive, I was certain that my appointment to manager might soon be called into question. I began to see myself as an unpopular and uninvited outsider. And so it was, that for the first time in many years, Mother's warnings rang in my daily thoughts once again.

Nevertheless, I hastily formulated a plan. I believed that if I could force heirs and stockholders to recognize my worth, then my position and title would be secure. I chose to do this by increasing the mill's operations. Of course, to expand operations, additional capital would be needed.

To increase my value, I hastily negotiated a line of credit with First Bank of Norfolk. I assured the bank that I had such authority, and I remained unstoppable in my persistence. The loan was secured by the equity of the Wells Lumber Mill No. 2, and I set forth to increase its profits exponentially. Regardless, soon after the shareholders learned of the loan obligation, and within three months of Mr. Well's passing I was removed from my position of manager.

Although I believed that I could provide adequate justification to all stockholders of Wells Company, I was never given such benefit. It was believed that I had mismanaged the mill and clearly exceeded my authority. The loan, itself, was absolved, but the accompanying fines were levied against the mill.

No effort was made to try me criminally, but stockholders brought court action to obtain repayment for the fines levied against the mill. Exhaustive efforts were made to ensure that I, personally, pay off the resulting bank fines and levies. The savings that I had so sparingly accumulated were now exhausted. My reputation and standing in the community were also ruined.

It seemed that the dark memory of these events would follow me to the grave. As my father warned, wickedness and wealth were, indeed, close associates. The world had seized my hopes and soon delegated me to my unavoidable rank. It was true that people like me were ill designed for success.

With my savings account bare and my reputation destroyed, I wandered aimlessly. I believed with all certainty of heart that I was a man of ill fortune destined to live a life of anguish and abject failure. Unable to work for Wells Company, I searched elsewhere for labor but was unsuccessful for quite a time.

Eventually, when the rumors and mumblings of my discharge had quieted, I was hired as a day carpenter for a man named Hiedwig. As an able worker I could have served Mr. Hiedwig well, but I did not. Of course, I remembered that a person might ascend through the ranks by hard work and persistence, but I began to believe that such efforts were futile and worthless. Imagine if you were once the esteemed manager of the largest mill in Virginia. Could you stomach working again as a day laborer? How would these painful memories, the foreman's whistle and the slurs of fellow laborers affect your spirit? What might you have felt?

# CHAPTER SIX

# How Impossible is Your Giant?

THE YEAR WAS 1881, AND MY THOUGHTS WERE dominated by a single conviction: the unfairness of my circumstance. Continual paintings of my dreadful past occupied the confines of my mind. As these memories occupied my daily thoughts, they changed my beliefs about the world and about me. Within a short time I had lost not only the desire I once had, but a part of me seemed to be slipping away. Unable to release myself from negative thought and belief, my mind and body began a slow, yet perceptible, decay.

Was I not mistaken that years of work could easily be taken away by the stroke of pen or by the whim of a wealthy inheritor? Should I be so foolish to again accept the idea that diligent effort could provide happiness, promotion or security? If I was to be cheated from my just payment, then was it not my responsibility to even the accounts?

Almost instantly, my mind began to search for means by which I could meet this goal, and I soon found ways to even the imbalance between myself and Mr. Hiedwig. To do this, I sought to obtain more compensation, yet provide less service. I began to work my craft at an unhurried pace and sat idle whenever possible. This desire to obtain more payment for less service soon became a dominating thought. At times, I also found my thoughts drawn toward acts of minor theft. Unable to devote my hands and heart to honest labor, comfort was found in the devilish fervor of lifting small articles of tools and provisions from old man Hiedwig. Albeit the articles stolen were petty, in the beginning, such acts brought me sadness and pain. But, soon, I considered this thievery fair, proper and even reassuring.

Twilight hours were spent seeking comfort in the taverns and rum houses near the waterfront. Many of these patrons were like me, hard working, but now cheated by the world and its selfish inhabitants. Indeed, in this group I resurrected ideas that I had discarded. As my new associates told of a higher order and of invisible systems that limited advancement and opportunity, I eagerly listened and absorbed each word.

And so it appeared a happenstance that, in spite of where I traveled or what quarter I visited, cohorts in the same or worse condition as I, came forward. Each of these men and women complained of the same impediments. All of them had discovered that every employer was a crook. Countless stories, tales and musings recounted how the shopkeeper's only aspiration was to cheat the worker from his earnings. Slowly, I found myself agreeing and affirming these ideas. The more I thought about them, the more my daily life supported their truth. My mental power became magnetized toward one simple dominating belief: Life is unfair and any honest effort will only be exploited.

As my thoughts and conditions descended, more companions with similar or worse circumstances surfaced. I never thought much about it at the time, but it was quite astounding how people of similar thoughts seemed to magically converge all around me. It was as if we were all swept up and gathered together by a giant invisible hand. In the grimy air of the rum houses and alleys, we assembled. Once gathered, I chanted the words of my father, "Wickedness and wealth are close associates!" Upon hearing this, the ruffians, crooks and drunkards would revel, waive their hook-shaped hands and cheer this rousing cry.

As weeks passed, I continued to expect greater payment from Mr. Hiedwig, but, at the same time, I provided less service. If Hiedwig was lucky and I unfortunate, it seemed perfectly fitting to even the scales of fortune. As such, my acts of thievery and idleness in the workplace continued, and soon I was without employment.

My body and mind continued to slip, as if my very existence was falling from a steep precipice into a dark chasm. At first, I lost a mere foothold, but then the momentum produced by my thoughts and deeds only cast me further down into the abyss. With little money for rent, I soon had no lodging. I lived on boulevard corners, in the dark alleys and at the alehouses. I then sought to charm lady luck and began street gambling. When all my coins were lost, I borrowed money from an unsavory and deadly character named Karvash. Within three days, gambling did consume this money, as well.

I soon turned to begging for my sustenance and the only reasonable way to repay my gambling debt. As I continued to decline, my contempt for the world and its appointed inheritors of success multiplied. The greedy heirs of Mr. Wells, the exploitation from Hiedwig, the inadequate charity from passers-by, and my gaming debts were all symbols of the same forces which sought to destroy unfortunate men such as myself.

At the depths of my fall, I awoke as a man of a wretched and ghastly sort. The gracious hands that fed me, I could only greet with a scowl. Since most of the coins I received were routinely stolen from my hands and pockets, I begged for food. As men sought my life for unpaid gambling debts, I lived and moved in great fear. I became a man of hollow innards, an empty vessel, with little understanding of the grave circumstances that encircled me.

Conventions of day and night, calendar months and years, were of little use to me now. The passage of time hastened, but remained incredibly slow. The course of day seemed to continue for an eternity, yet years would pass in rapid succession. I cannot say how much time did, indeed, pass until one windy, dark night I learned the year was 1885, and the month December. To my reckoning, nearly five years had passed in a manner that could be described only as inhuman. Thievery and utter violence encircled my proximity at all times. While I routinely paid Karvash and his gang what little I could, I knew that my time would soon run out. I might die from the ravages of cold, hunger, or by Karvash's reptilian hand; his icy blade piercing my throat.

ON THE NIGHT OF DECEMBER 27, 1885, I walked the same streets that I traveled on the morning of my arrival many years before. I thought, perhaps, a part of me might still be found by re-tracing these steps. People in all manner of dress and temperament passed me by. I looked upon them all, but each man, woman, and child looked away. Carriages wheeled by me without regard for my proximity, and I nearly met my fate under their giant creaking wheels. To the world, it seemed that I was invisible, a non-entity.

Heavy, dark clouds began to assemble, and soon they rolled across the twilight sky like a battalion of invaders. Their chilling winds began to whirl paper, debris and dust all around me, as I oscillated along my path. Thunder rumbled in the distance, and the streets soon became noiseless and empty. The temperature was dropping rapidly and I knew that a significant, winter storm would arrive quickly. Blasts of wind and heavy rain strewn me about and I picked up my steps along the lifeless streets. I retreated back to my familiar alleyway and sat my shivering, wet body on the grimy, alley floor. An initial bolt of lightning lit up the sky overhead, then another and another. During one of the flashes, my eyes were pointed toward my lower quarters. In an instant, the torn, filthy pants, dusty legs and withered condition startled me. They were atrocious; they were my own. At this moment, my desolation became astonishingly clear and my condition seemingly impossible.

I vowed that here I would breathe my last breath; that I would leave the vile circumstances that ensnared me.

"It seemed the red-faced man in the saloon was right many years ago," I reasoned to myself. "Perhaps I was of the same weak and feeble temperament as my father. Perchance, Mother was quite feeble, as well, and this is why she expired so quickly."

And so it seemed that the fate of my father and mother had finally caught up to me. I decided that I would simply allow it to devour me.

I would never arise again. I shall perish in the darkness of the night. Whatever volition remained in my mind and body, I closed my eyes and centered my energies to this end. By sheer mercy, I hoped that this wish would be fulfilled.

# CHAPTER SEVEN

# Encased in this Crypt

THE STORM INTENSIFIED AS AN ARCTIC STREAM OF wind and icy rain battered the northern side of the ten-story mercantile building. Having positioned my body on its south side, I was sheltered from the frigid winds that penetrated the city that night. Cocooned in a small corner of a forgotten dark alleyway, my body was surrounded on all sides by magnificent edifices of brick, mortar and plaster. I closed my eyes and lay down on the damp floor. For a moment, my mind was silent, yet, soon, impulses of thought did spring forward from the deep, subconscious sections of my psyche and I was struck for an instant with a haunting question:

"Had I bargained life away for a slight pittance, for nothing?"

Often, a brief shelter from the mauling wind or falling rain would bring some contentment to me. Yet, tonight, I felt none and could only ask myself, "Had I been cheated, or was I the cheater?"

As if to propel myself back to my grim reality, I opened my eyes slightly. The misery of my current circumstances quickly put an end to all questions. Again, I heard the barrage of hammering winds and the icy rain. I listened to the rattle and ring of wandering glass bottles set into motion by the windstorm. I inhaled the stench of the rotting rubbish and refuse surrounding me. I saw two large, black rats scurry across my line of vision. One had a scaly tail which trailed behind it. The other had none. Again, I sank down into my familiar logic.

And then, like clockwork, I returned to my own dire reality. Once again, my beliefs and my world were comfortably guided by my current condition and the physical senses. "No more inquiries" I said to myself, "no more inquiries."

In that moment, I found a hollow relief in the powerless, the incapable, and the fallacy of surrender. As I lay trembling on the cold, cobblestone floor of the alley, I waited for death to overtake me. Encased in this crypt, I felt as an ant among giants, alone and forgotten.

# CHAPTER EIGHT

# A Crushing Giant

FREEZING WIND AND RAIN CONTINUED TO bombard the city. While I was protected from these external elements, there was another storm from which I seemed incapable of escaping. The misery of my circumstance and my seeming helplessness bombarded my mind with a ferocity that surpassed even that of the rainstorm.

I slipped into a brief sleep but was soon awakened. Some may not believe the story I am now about to tell. Yet, I had visions that night that were so genuine to my eyes and senses, that I can only say they were absolutely real. Before proceeding, I must also warn that, to some, the following account may be quite disturbing.

I was awakened by a presence that arose from my very core and only later entered my sight. At first, there were the traditional feelings and rumblings of sorrow that I had grown accustomed to. Yet, as this force grew closer, these pains swelled to an unbearable sort. An unfathomable and incessant agony penetrated every part of my person, and soon my entire spirit seemed suffocated by its power. Gloom of a bottomless and most horrendous nature overtook my entire being, such that I had little doubt that I was in the presence of a destructive and evil force of the highest order.

The force was not a man, but stood towering above me as an enormous dark figure. It had no shape and no form, yet it spanned from the cobblestone floor of the alley to a height of ten feet or more! It had neither arms nor legs. It had neither a head nor shoulders. As it came to me in the dead of the night, it was much more than a shadow. A scholar of such things I am not; yet, I can now say that it was a force of emptiness and fear.

To me, it seemed an impossible foe, so consuming and overwhelming that I began to sob uncontrollably and shake frantically. Horror and sadness grew within my mind and, almost immediately, the immense darkened form enlarged again. The form grew to fifteen feet in height, then to twenty feet, and then to thirty feet! Immediately, a crushing giant stood before me! Paralyzed by fear and numbed by the cold, I lay on the icy, wet bricks, awaiting the death I so invited.

As I waited for my inevitable fate, another visitor came forward. From the foot of the immense, darkened force came the outline of a wretched being, a tiny creature. As this second visitor inched toward me, the howling wind and rain continued to increase in intensity. As it neared, I could clearly see that it was the form of a man. Yet, it was not an ordinary man, but one of undersized proportion. As this miniscule caller came into focus, my fears continued to multiply. As my terror increased and expanded, the darkened figure continued to grow and inflate in all directions. This menacing form now stood to nearly one hundred feet and had tremendous width. It now eclipsed the top and east side of the mercantile building.

Extraordinarily, the second caller hardly sprouted from the ground! As my face lay trembling against the chilly, cobblestone floor, I noticed that this miniature being was now crouched in fear, and its back was facing me. This dreadful being could not have been more than one foot in height and was a shameful display. It had no garments of any kind, yet, it was covered with a thick coat of filth and grime. Its form was grotesquely emaciated, and its bones, veins and vessels stood out in bold prominence. Where flesh could be seen, its color was gray, bruised and bloodied. Perhaps, most disturbing, its skin seemed to drip from its bones, and a clear stench of death accompanied it.

As I viewed this sight and smelled its odor, I could not move or articulate a sound. The visions I saw produced a reaction of fear that was unspeakable. Even more pronounced, was the continued domination of the darkened force. I can say with all certainty that, as my fears grew, this darkened force continued to expand in all directions.

An ever-deepening misery continued to encase and overwhelm me. It was a torment not known to this world. Imagine the terror of falling without end. While falling, I felt my essence becoming smaller and smaller in size, and a bitter darkness overtaking me.

At a time when I believed that my fear had reached an unbearable level, another astounding, yet terrifying, realization was about to occur.

# CHAPTER NINE
## Into the Cracks

As I DIMINISHED, THE SHADOWY FORCE continued to swell to monstrous proportions. The figure now covered the mercantile building, the Federal Custom House, and all other buildings around me. Soon, the gas lamps glowing at the end of each block grew dim, and I saw each flame gasp its last breath. Then, this darkened figure began to consume the remaining light immediately around me.

Surrounded in every direction, I now saw a curtain of complete darkness. Most terrifying of all, I felt this destructive presence continue to overtake every living cell within me. If I was once an ant among giants, I was now but a mere microbe cast into the cracks of civilization. My strongest wish was to disappear, to cease my existence, to never have been born.

I began to plead for leniency and sympathy. I begged with every ounce of my heart for these ghastly episodes to end. As if to indicate that there would be no sympathy, no reprieve, no end, a most dreadful revelation occurred next. The tiny visitor at the foot of the enormous shadowy force revealed to me its own terrifying secret! A blanket of deeper shock and disgust engulfed me as my eyes focused in on the sight before me. It caused me to reach a height of fear so elevated that I cannot fathom how I did, in fact, survive.

The ghastly gray-fleshed visitor turned its head to reveal its face. Imagine the horror when I realized that its hideous face was, indeed, my very own!

At this moment, I wished beyond any desire imaginable that I could change my previous actions; that I could somehow start anew. In the years since my dismissal from Wells Company, I had become downtrodden and defeated. Yet, could my fate have been different? Might I have continued forward?

My senses could no longer partake in the events I was experiencing. I tightly closed my eyes and covered my ears. My physical organs were pounding in fear and my body cavities shook. I believed with certainty that I would soon expire from the complete shock of this unimaginable episode.

# CHAPTER TEN
# *Cold and Motionless*

CONTINUALLY, THE IMAGES OF THESE VISITORS raced about my mind. The pounding of my heart created an intolerable echo in my skull as a deep misery overtook me. Thoughts of my birth into poverty, my tragic childhood and my past failures all haunted my mind, without end. As my fears rose to a level of hysteria, the howling wind became deafening.

My physical body felt as if, at any moment, it would be pulled apart in all directions. I lay on the cold and wet alley floor, curled like a tightly-wound knot. My only recourse was to cover my ears, strain my eyes shut and wait for the inevitable end.

Amidst this violent storm, a single question came forward: Was I still alive? I pinched my skin hard and felt a sharp sting of pain. Indeed, I was still quite alive.

As all things do, my newest revelation started as something very small. It began as a tiny particle, or a fragment of an idea. Yet, as I focused on it, this tiny thought particle grew. And, in a short time, incredible ideas now stretched and vibrated across the caverns of my once-uncontrolled thinking. From the depths of my mind, these questions presented themselves:

> **"If I am still alive, then am I stronger than this darkened form? And, if I am stronger than it, why do I have so much fear?"**

As I asked these questions, another illumination came forward and filled my thoughts:

> **"If I fear something that I can survive, then I must be operating from a lesser part of my being."**

I reasoned then, that there must be another part of me; a part which is greater and stronger. Then something told me that no matter the intensity of hunger in my belly, the cold blistering of my skin, or the giant in my path, I still retained possession of my mind. I still had the ability to choose my thoughts. And it was at this moment that my final desire was born. It was to outlast the adversity of this moment, and for the first time in many years, I stopped thinking about my fears. The storm quieted.

I found myself reflecting on times when I believed myself more than able to take on any task. In a short passage of time, perhaps a minute or two, my deep gloom and desperation subsided. The once-screaming wind also diminished to that of a dull murmur. The shackles of fear and anxiety that bound me for years seemed to, temporarily, loosen their claws.

With my eyes tightly closed, I lay cold and motionless. From somewhere deep in my mind, the memories of my first days in Virginia came forward. I do not recall why I dwelled on these events, but they seemed to give me some comfort. Perhaps, they were a pleasurable escape from the years of worry and fear that had consumed me. My mind drifted until I saw and felt my first days in Virginia before me, once again. I vividly saw the bustling port on a clear, blue, October morning. I inhaled the fresh winds as they kissed my skin. I listened to the sweet cacophony of merchants, tradesmen and others scurrying about. I saw the boundless beauty of human creation, movement and might, all before me, once again.

I began to feel the same immeasurable pride that I held in such days. For the first time in many years, I lay in peace, yet, there was no way to prepare for the astonishing sight that would soon greet me.

## CHAPTER ELEVEN

# Proceed Without Delay!

As MY THOUGHTS CONTINUED, THE MURMURING winds quieted. Then my ears began to hear the recurrent tapping of quick footsteps coming closer. I should have felt fear, yet, these footsteps had a differing affect on my spirit. Whereas the dark force produced a deepening gloom, these footsteps raised in me a buoyant sentiment. As these steps came closer, oh how these feelings grew stronger! Where doubt and confusion once stood, I felt brief flashes of conviction and certainty. Where terror and loathing once dwelled, love and confidence seemed to come forward.

I opened my eyes, startled to discover a greeter who displayed a powerful magnetism and constituted an amazing vision. It stood, perhaps, 25 feet from me, and was a sharp contrast to the ghastly displays which I had seen on this night. The caller resembled a man in formal attire and donned a medium-height, black top hat, a long, wool, frock coat and carried an ornate, brass-handled, walking cane. A glowing, white chemise set off its black, velvet vest. This visitor stood in an erect and certain manner, and had an aura which seemed to elevate the world around it. It was a dazzling display.

Although it stood looking at me for a time, I turned my head away, in shame. Then, its thundering voice echoed through the alley:

"Rouse yourself from this feeble condition! Awaken now, proceed without delay!" it commanded.

I drew my head higher and looked its way again. I could see the cadence of its quick steps and its top hat rhythmically flowing higher and lower. It was coming closer!

As the figure drew nearer, my mind reeled in shock. Imagine my surprise when I began to notice a most unusual aspect of its appearance, perhaps the most astounding sight I had seen, thus far. Its face seemed to be clearly that of a man, but I could not identify just one man. It may be truthful to say that it was one being or force, but many faces. I can only describe its facial features as changing from the expression of one individual to another. I could, at times, discern one head, yet many altering appearances. While I had little fear of this caller, I still sat timidly, with my knees held tightly to my chest.

As it neared the spot where I rested, I could see that it bore the expression of a confident man of an age perhaps similar to my own. It displayed a lifted brow, a slight nose and a distinguished moustache. Yet, amazingly, its features then transformed to that of a dignified man of elder years, with a powerful, bearded chin and piercing eyes. **Then, its features changed again, and then again!** All images, indeed, were different, yet strikingly similar; how peculiar this scene was!

I was reminded of a man I once viewed on a discarded newssheet. As I huddled in an alleyway one cold night, I came across a newspaper containing the picture of a man of great wealth, named 'Carnegie'. The same man it was not, but this new caller had a commanding presence similar to what I sensed from the paper rendering. It had a unity of mind and purpose that I also noticed in men like Mr. Wells. No matter the variation, it was clear that a single current or force did etch its features, its magnetism, and its essence.

## Chapter Twelve

# I Am the You!

AGAIN, THE DEEP AND COMPELLING VOICE commanded:

"Rouse yourself from this feeble condition! Awaken now, proceed without delay!"

My hands trembled. I raised my head up for an instant, only to drop down again in disgrace. The caller addressed me once more, and somehow I knew that it would not take indolence as a response:

"William Boyle, do rouse yourself and cast this specter of fear from our presence!"

My heart pounded and I found myself in complete astonishment that this caller could know my name. How could it have learned of a ragged street dweller like me, so consumed by fear and living out an unfortunate existence? In shock of this revelation, I cried out:

**"Please Sir, reveal to me who you may be?"** I asked in a guarded, but feverish, pitch.

"I am the you that could have been, the you that may still be. I am the you who does not know of self-created fear, doubt and limitation."

At this moment, I believed that my existence had, indeed, reached its final conclusion. I suspected that, somehow, I was walking into another dreadful doorway, a passageway into another hellish world. I was certain that, at any second, this sordid plot would conclude with my dreadful end! I crouched again in fear, with my head planted between my knees, and remained shaking for a time.

# CHAPTER THIRTEEN
# The Amazing Journey Begins...

I BEGAN TO FEAR THAT IF I CAST MY SIGHTS AGAIN on this caller, its form might change to that of a hideous beast or the shadowy figure. A space of time passed until I drew the courage to raise my head and direct my eyes, once again, toward it.

The caller was standing erect and strong with a purposeful, yet patient, look about its expression. Viewing its countenance somehow provided me with a level of security. Again, I asked the figure of its origin.

**"P-please Sir, may you disclose who you are?"** I pleaded anxiously.

"As I have said, William, I am the he that is in you," the caller responded, gracefully.

This was an impossible statement to accept, so I cried out, **"Please stop tormenting me! I am left with nothing but my decaying self. I have lost all will!"**

The caller responded, with sincerity, "Why do you misjudge your wealth, for I am all that you may still become. At any time you desire, you may take possession of your world and command it to be so."

And so it was that the amazing journey would begin. It continued until every doubt was removed and the wisdom of antiquity became obvious and simple. Here are the events and discourse that transpired on that incredible night in 1885. As you travel with us, do not be surprised or frightened if someone within you comes forward and connects with the caller's words:

**"With respect dear Sir, I do not have your strength and, therefore, could never be like you. Moreover, Sir, our faces are quite different. How then?"** I asked the caller.

"I no longer look like you because you have removed me from your thinking. Because of this, I take not your form, but the form of others you saw who connected with my power. I am the last connection of your thoughts to your true self, your creative self."

**"Your facial features..."** I quickly bit my words and wished that I could gobble them from the air.

"Why do my facial features transform? Is this what you are trying to ask?"

With clasped hands and my head bowed, I whispered, **"My apologies, dear Sir, for my questions."**

"Do not be apologetic! My face changes appearance because you have so forgotten this side of yourself. Since you have abandoned me, only brief images of what you saw in others becomes my form. Since your thoughts are erratic and weak, your vision of me fades and changes. However, my essence always remains the same."

The caller's voice grew louder and it startled me, "Listen closely!" it commanded. "You have weakened your true self in favor of something that is not worthy of you. You are serving your false self."

# CHAPTER FOURTEEN

# Two Selves Live inside You

I WAS SO PERPLEXED BY THESE SUGGESTIONS that I could hardly assemble the words to speak. How could this caller be connected to me? What was a creative self? I doubted that its words were true, so I asked the caller in a low and inhibited tone:

**"You speak of a true self and a false self, but I am one person. Why do you trick me so?"**

"It is no trick. Every man and woman is a plurality of person. Your body is only the dwelling place where these two selves live. Do not let this fact escape you, for it is the true reality of all human condition.

"One self you may identify as your true self, your creative self or your higher self. You may call it whatever you wish, but it is connected to a higher wisdom, to greater sources of guidance, and is one with everything else in the Universe. It is connected to all things. It is only this true self which can deliver real happiness, peace, and abundance. This is the person you were created to be, and the person that you dream about becoming in quiet times and during your grandest moments. In fact, I am the one who sends you these dreams and desires, the visions of a future that can be yours. If you take hold of this power it will be yours."

**"Then, Sir, what is the other self?"** I inquired.

"The other self is your lesser self, your false self. It was created by your ego, and is a misapplication of your true power."

**"Please, Sir, if this is true, then where does this destructive self come from? What is it?"**

"This lesser self is created by your ego and the incorrect notion that you are separate from all things. It is destructive and it grows whenever you forget your connection to something greater than you and to your true self.

"So, this false self will slowly begin to rule your life. When you fail to act from a higher a higher consciousness, it grows. It can even fool you into believing that it will protect you! In reality, it will only oppose the true self and your own happiness."

At that moment, I remembered the first two callers I had seen earlier in the night. A chill ran up my spine at the notion of these things, and I wanted nothing more than to run away from it all. Yet, from somewhere, burning questions came forward.

**"Sir, if two selves live in me, then how can they be so different?"**

"Understand this fact: One self shall connect you to all goodness, power, intelligence and peace. The other self may only lay ruin to your mind and body.

"When instruction from your creative self is followed, the destructive self is minimized. When instruction from the lesser self is followed, your connection with your true self is minimized and, soon, the person you were meant to become drifts further away.

"These two selves compete for the attention of your mind and body. Realize this, and you shall begin to understand the secret workings of the world around you."

# CHAPTER FIFTEEN

# A Fragment to be Hurled Aside

I CONTINUED TO ASK THIS CALLER QUESTION after question. It seemed that, before me lay a deep wisdom and, no matter how peculiar its source, I must listen. Questions continued to flow from my mind in a nearly unending fashion:

**"Dear Sir, I certainly hope that you do not tire of my questioning. But if two selves exist, then why do I not see them in myself, and in others? Where are they now?"**

The caller pointed toward the open thoroughfare beyond the alleyway, and said, "Indeed they are visible for all who care to look."

I began to wonder if I had lost my sanity. Surely, two selves were never visible to me. All of this was too much for my mind to accept and I began to think of it as an amusing tale, but nothing more. Realizing my disbelief, the caller addressed me in a more commanding tone:

"You will see the manifestations of these two selves, or entities, all around you. A person who serves the false self will find his attention directed toward the things he does not want. Thus, where you see lack, insecurity, jealousy, fear and hopelessness, the destructive self has become this person's master.

"It is also true that, where you see real happiness, abundance, strength, confidence, well-being and peace, you will find those who have chosen to follow their creative self. It is only this creative self that can connect you to who you were created to become."

In a powerful tone, and with its eyes directed and fixed upon me, the caller said, "Examine your own life and then ponder which self has ruled over your thoughts, beliefs and actions."

I took no time to ponder, but cried out in worry, **"Sir, Sir! Did I witness these entities on this long night? What do you know of the dark shadowy figure?"**

"Yes, indeed, you did. You saw the very world that you had created through your own thoughts and beliefs. You were given a rare glimpse of the unyielding forces you allowed to guide your life."

The caller looked at me sternly and asked, "You witnessed a darkened shadowy force which brought emptiness and fear, correct?"

Another bout of fright overtook me as I realized this visitor knew of the ghastly sights I had seen earlier in the night. I cautiously looked to my left and right, and then in a soft whisper said,

**"Y-yes, I did, Sir."**

"This figure is your destructive self, your lesser self. You may call it whatever you choose, but it is your weakened entity. Every man or woman sometimes loses control to this self, for brief moments. Yet, you have given it far too much power in recent years!"

"You see, this false self was not always so large, and it was not always your master. There was another time in your life when it could never overshadow who you were destined to become, it could never overshadow the real you."

I could hardly assemble the words to speak. Certainly, I would never create such a monster. I reasoned that: perhaps this night was only a bad dream, or perchance these visions were created by my imagination. Yet, almost immediately, a whisper crept from my mouth,

**"Sir, the gray-fleshed and weakened caller, what of it?"**

"The ghastly miniature being who crouched in fear, you ask?" the caller replied, loudly.

**"Yes, the miniature, bloodied creature. It was a figment of my imagination, correct?"** I asked softly.

"No, it was absolutely real!" responded the caller. "This miserable wretch always lives below the shadowy figure. The self-defeating talk and negative beliefs you lavish upon yourself can only come from this part of you."

**"Sir, it cannot be!"** I cried out, no longer in a whisper. **"But who caused its bruises and bloodied its skin?"**

In a thunderous and commanding tone, the caller set forth its decisive answer, "Why, the only one with the power to do such a thing. The only one who could create its scars and starve its power, you! You minimized yourself and bloodied your flesh. Its form is an exact reflection of your destructive thought habits. You famished and tortured it, day-by-day and hour-by-hour. It is an exact reflection of the world you chose to create within you and around you."

**"Oh, dear Sir, these things haunt me!"** I whimpered. My hands were now feverishly rubbing my eyes and face. **"Please tell me that the gray-fleshed, weakened creature was not me!"**

"If you do not want to listen, should I lie to increase your comfort?  Do you want to live blind to the world in and around you?"

The caller leaned forward and then looked at me intently, "Realize that I once connected with you and guided your thoughts. The miniature, bloodied creature once stood strong, just as I do now!"

I reeled in complete shock of the revelation now before me. Yet, quickly, a flash of doubt came forward, and I asked,

**"If this is true, then why didn't I see you below the shadowy figure?"**

With this suggestion, the caller let out a loud and roaring laugh.  It was as if I had spoken of a most ridiculous suggestion, something foolish and absolutely impossible.

A wide smile covered its face and it grew taller, broader in stature.  "The shadowy force would be crushed at my heel, or perhaps even too infinitesimal to even crush!  When I exist fully and completely in you, this shadowy form is dwarfed by even the most tiny, microscopic speck.  It is a water molecule to the vast ocean."

**"Then where were you when the shadowy figure loomed over me? Why did you not protect me?"** I protested in anger.

"I cannot connect to the mind of one who thinks of defeat, lack or failure.  When you blame others for your situation, or when you act in a manner unlike your true self, you cannot hear me. Once you became pre-occupied with such things, I could not connect with your mind any longer."

**"B-but, Sir, I do not understand"** I blurted out.

"Make no mistake," the caller said, looking toward the area where the wretched being once squirmed, "that gray and bloodied wretch is you, as you grovel and crawl in thought each day. As you see within, you can only create on the outside."

Fear of a terrible sort overtook me, and I cried out, **"Sir, please tell me then, how can I stop the shadowy force from devouring me!"**

The caller crept closer to me, and with its face nearly twelve inches from mine, it whispered, "If you learn nothing else, realize this one fact: *It is only you* who believe yourself too weak, too unlucky and too poor."

The caller resumed its normal tone and stepped away from me. "If you would exercise your inherited power, the dark shadow would be nothing but an infinitesimal fragment, hurled aside by the miraculous giant that is you! *You see, I know who you are, and who you are supposed to become.*"

# CHAPTER SIXTEEN
# You Can Leave This Place!

THE CALLER CONTINUED TO ADDRESS ME WITH AN air of confidence and security. All the while, its facial appearance seemed to transform and transmute into different people. Each face radiated an unstoppable assurance, a harmony and a love to the world around it. As any person might be, I was shocked by the spectacle. Perhaps more importantly, however, I was mesmerized by its accounts, and felt my spirits ascending. Our discussions continued:

"William, when you decided to leave New York, your destructive self was reduced to a tiny crumb, perchance like a grain of sand. It was a mere speck, which did not occupy your consciousness. You followed my urges and, lo, you advanced!

"Yet, when you were dismissed from Wells Company, you questioned my command and abandoned me. You began to dwell upon thoughts of weaknesses, fear and hopelessness.

"And, soon, your false self grew and it could only destroy. You nurtured it as a farmer cultivates his crops. At all hours, you concentrated on thoughts that fed and fortified it. You gave it your power and it grew. Soon, you accepted more and more destructive thoughts and these became your new beliefs. As you gave me little attention, I, your creative self, diminished in your day-to-day life. As I cannot dwell in a polluted-thought world, you forced me outside of your awareness."

**"Then why do you come to me now?"**

"You changed your thoughts briefly and brought me, again, to your own awareness. If I did not come to you at this time, then the false destructive self would have ended your life. You certainly would have been destroyed in due time or, perhaps, on this very night. Yet, when you recounted times in which you were in harmony, brave, or acting with great faith, you called me forward, and together we began again. Do you remember a change in your thoughts?"

**"Indeed, I do, Sir. It was the only thing that stopped the incessant pain which I felt."**

"Of course!" said the caller. It looked at me blankly and continued, "Please mark these words well: this destructive self will trick you into believing that it is acting for your protection. Know that this is a lie, because, if left uncontrolled, it will see you to an early end. Its harvest is your own destruction."

I swallowed hard, **"S-sir, did you say that its harvest will be my early death?"**

"Yes, without question!" the caller said mechanically. "This false self can only create limitation, lack and misery. The false or destructive self can only suppress you in your journey to who you are promised to become. It can only remove happiness, destroy your expansion, and vanquish self worth. Remember these words well and never forget them: Your false self can only lead you to decline and, if allowed to run rampant, self annihilation."

Regardless of the caller's admonitions, I could not imagine that any force would seek to destroy me. Yet, I could not deny the great pain I felt in recent years. It seemed that something had ensnared me, and that I could not break free from it.

**"S-sir,"** I replied, my hands now trembled in fear, **"is control of these fates even possible?"**

"Listen closely: Choice of which self you direct your attention to is under your complete control. No matter the circumstance, you, right now, at this moment, have complete control.

"It may not appear so, but thoughts are always your property and always your dominion. Just as bricks, mortar and stone are implements to the mason, thoughts are tools for the creation of your vast kingdom.

"With this control of thought, you have power over which entity you direct your attention to."

**"W-why is this thought power under each person's control?"** I asked, with hands still shaking from fear.

"Thought provides each person with the power to create or change their destiny at will. It is the most important power of all humankind. Yet, it is squandered and wasted by deeply held fears, guilt and resentment."

It all seemed so strange to me. I felt like a visitor trying to learn an entire language, or perhaps an entire culture, in one sitting. I wondered why such truths had eluded me for all of these years. Were such things shielded from those with impoverished upbringings? Determined to find out why I lacked this knowledge, I asked more questions.

**"If one's thought has so much power, why wasn't I told of this earlier in my life?"**

"If you lack knowledge of these laws now, it is because you have chosen to ignore them. You were content to live without thinking of their power and function. Yet, even in your darkest hour, complete power has always been within your immediate grasp."

I blew warm air on my hands to remove the sting of the cold, and then asked, **"But, how can I be subject to these rules if I was never taught them?"**

"When you were a young child, you may not have known or understood the laws of gravitation. Nevertheless, you would have fallen to your death if dropped from above. These laws operate without regard to your knowledge of them, and they shall not yield to your current whims or lack of understanding.

"Ignorance shall not delay, diminish or divert their power, and, as with all laws, ignorance is no excuse."

**"Can my mind and its thought power help my current condition?"**

"Of course! In fact, your outward condition will never change until your inner condition is transformed. You see, at this very moment, there is something deep down inside of you, something that you greatly long for. Deep within you, there is a dream that you have abandoned. *This dream and desire is woven into who you are meant to become.* This dream is one with your true self; do not let it go!"

Again, I felt the grip of fear overwhelm me. How could I take control of anything at this moment? I could only assume that these laws would act against people like me.

Again, my hands and body began to shake and I cried out, **"Sir, oh, the misery of it all! Oh, why must this horrible reality be so?"**

"Stop dwelling on false information" the caller thundered. "In this instant, I am telling you, with all my power; *do not let go of your deepest desires!*

"There is only one you! In all of history, there has never been another, and no matter how many years we look forward, there will never be anyone like you. You are absolutely and inexorably unique. *There is a reason!*"

These words did little to ease my fear and worry. It seemed that the caller greatly misjudged me and my situation. Perhaps, it did not see the rags on my back and the alley that I occupied. I plunged to the floor at the caller's feet and began to sob. My body shivered, and I clenched tightly at its feet.

**"Oh, please, dear Sir, I am a sorrowful man in these years, living as a base animal with hunger, warmth and survival as my only aims; I cannot dwell on anything more!"**

The caller then tapped its brass handled cane swiftly on the ground three times, as if to ensure my attention was focused.

"Please understand this now: Your dominant consciousness creates your world! The world around you does not create your dominant consciousness."

Then, an unimaginable statement came from its lips, "Just as I told you in the saloon house many years ago, when you were a scared child, I am telling you here and now. *William, you can leave this place!*"

My mind could only hear what it wanted to accept hear and I snarled back in fury, **"Stop tricking me!"**

My hands then began to flutter uncontrollably, and I pounded my fists on the soggy floor, diffusing water all around me as I spoke.

**"You could not know my childhood sadness. Your riddles are nothing but lies!"**

I quickly lifted myself away from its feet and sat with my arms folded. The caller's words made little sense to me, and, perhaps worse, each explanation blamed me for the bad luck I faced in recent years. How could a person's outward condition be created by thought? I knew that my own condition was caused by the greedy heirs of Mr. Wells. Clearly, their injustice had created my surroundings on this very night.

I decided that I would no longer listen to its tales and partake in its mindless drivel.

I looked away from it, in anger.

# CHAPTER SEVENTEEN
# The Watchman at the Gate

To my amazement, the caller positioned its back towards me and I began to hear it walking away. I turned around and quickly raised myself from the cobblestone floor. I began to see the outline of its top hat and figure, in the distance. It was leaving the alley. Quickly, anger drowned my reason and I began to taunt it.

**"Oh, why are you leaving me, oh great exalted one?"** I asked in a sneering manner. The caller stopped for a moment, its kind tone offered a response,

"I told you earlier that I cannot live within the mind of one who thinks of defeat and blames others for their situation." With these words, the caller continued its departure.

Terror came upon me and my heart began to pound violently. I cried out, **"But, S-sir...I cannot survive much longer without you!"**

The alley was empty again. Everything around me now felt heavy, dark and stagnate. Again, I smelled the rotten odors. The weight of my circumstance and the cold of the night pressed upon me once more. Even the air seemed to push my body lower and lower toward the slimy, alley floor and the spot where I once lay. My head turned downward and my shoulders felt like enormous sand bags were tugging forcibly at them.

Through the deep fog of the night, I heard the whistle of a merchant ship moaning through the air, and I knew it was leaving its berth. I had seen many ships leave the port district. They might cross the Atlantic or travel northeast to another haven, never to return again. I looked up again but the caller was gone. The crying whistle of the departing ship cut through the deep fog one last time and my ears rang. At that moment, something deep inside of me stirred, and I yelled out:

**"Sir, wait...I have, for a brief time, dwelled on higher thoughts!"**

The caller did not return. Again, I dropped my head down in shame.

Although it seemed I had no strength left, from somewhere, power sprang forward in me. My legs coiled and I ran around the corner at full trot. The caller was walking briskly and far ahead of me. I stopped, perhaps 30 feet from it, and exclaimed:

**"Sir, I have, for a brief time, dwelled on higher things!"**

Tragically, there was no response.

I ran again, faster and harder, until I was alongside the caller. Then, almost immediately, its steps halted. I stopped, as well, and quickly found myself hunched over and catching my breath. The wintry night air stung my throat, and I panted. The caller seemed to be looking directly forward. As I raised my head, I was surprised at what I saw. Right in front of me stood a black, horse-drawn, Phaeton carriage.

The caller then climbed aboard the carriage and said, "You shall learn a great deal on this journey, if you choose to listen."

The caller grabbed the reins with its hands, as fear directed my eyes to the large wheels of the carriage. I remembered that similar creaking giants nearly crushed me earlier in the evening. I decided to let this strange visitor depart on its way.

More surprises lay in store for me because, from somewhere beyond my cognition, a flash of faith met with impulse. In an instant, my left shoe was planted on the carriage footstep. The caller's hands cast a deep ripple in the lengthy, leather reigns. The ripple ended its journey as a loud 'snap' against the horse's neck. I remember my body settling into the seat of the open carriage and hearing the heavy rhythmic clap of hooves against Main Street. I was in the carriage and we were moving!

**"Sir, where are we going?"**

"There is no destination, only a journey."

**"Sir, I tried to tell you that, for a brief time, I dwelled on higher thoughts. I tried, but the things I wanted never seemed to come."**

"Ever-changing desires, wishes or curiosity shall never result in the attainment of any lasting change. Although the journey of achievement begins with a spark of desire, this desire must be maintained.

"A great many things will cross your path on this night. Examples of success and failure, opportunity and lack, happiness and pain, always surround you. You must first accept these truths before you can see the secret world that operates outside of your awareness."

**"Sir, I do want to understand the world and I have dwelled on many higher thoughts. Why didn't my circumstances change?"** I asked enthusiastically.

The caller responded in a calm and careful tone, "You must concentrate on what you want with all of your attention and will. It has been many years since you acted in this manner.

"Remember, all people have numerous wishes and idle hopes, but only a few can identify what they truly want. Even fewer can hold on to it. Set yourself as different from the horde. Know exactly what you desire from the deepest part of your being. Ignite this desire, act upon it and never release it. Then, what the world claims is impossible, may certainly become yours!"

The dark and ominous clouds over our heads quickly rolled across the night sky like floating mountains. Forceful blasts of steam surged from the horse's nostrils, as we moved forward. As the carriage began to approach the intersection of Main and Concord Street, for whatever reason, I slowly turned my head to look at the caller. Unlike my own breath, and even that of the horse, I saw no wisps of steam coming from its nose and mouth!

It was quite a shocking sight, indeed, and I was beside myself with astonishment. It felt like my skin and bones wanted to leap from the very bench where I sat! It was only my mind that wanted to stay, and somehow it reasoned that if this caller had great knowledge, I should learn more. Would you have done the same? Only you can answer, but just as your curiosity continues, so did mine. My questions persisted:

**"Sir, please tell me more about these two selves."**

"A battle rages in your mind and in the minds of all people. Do not forget that there are two selves inside of you. There is your true self and your destructive self. The true self is connected to all

66

power. There is also a destructive self that is connected to all weakness and all fear; the absence of forgiveness and the abandonment of wisdom. Both fight for your attention. Remember these things!" the caller implored.

Indeed, these words made more sense to me, but as you can understand, I found it hard to believe that any battle raged inside me.

The carriage was now stopped along Main Street. The glow of a nearby street lamp saturated the open air around us, with a yellow haze. In this glow, I began to feel alive and expectant, and very different than I had felt in many years. Perhaps, as you might have done, I continued with my questions:

**"What does this creative self have to do with desire, Sir?"**

"All people wish or hope for more happiness or for a better life. But wishes and flickering hopes never allow you to put aside your limitations and to truly connect with me."

**"What limitations are you speaking of?"** I asked in a perplexed tone.

"Each person has created or accepted beliefs about themselves and their world. These beliefs form a set of rules and they create each person's life experience. Most will carry around limiting rules for their entire lives. They believe what they were told as children or what society tells them they cannot be. They live their entire lives, afraid to transcend these rules. These rules are called your beliefs. These beliefs can limit your connection to me and limit your connection to your true power. Like a mighty elephant held back by only a thin piece of twine, most people cage themselves until the day they physically die."

**"Why are people unable to connect with this power?"**

"William, most people's minds are divided. They are divided in thought between what they wish for and the worry, insecurities and limiting beliefs that frighten them."

**"So a person must not be divided in thought?"** I said, still trying to assimilate all before me, **"Why is this so?"**

"Most people will hold a desire for only a brief time. They will, then, invariably devote equal attention to their destructive self. And, just as the creation process begins, it soon ends. You see, the creative self will work within all the forces of nature to make one's desire a reality. Yet, the great forces will never be realigned and re-ordered according to whims and the weak hopes of a divided mind. It is only a specific, deep and overwhelming desire to break past your fears, cast away imaginary limitations, and hold focused thought and action that will allow one to connect with my power."

**"Please Sir, tell me more!"** I requested hungrily.

"When the desire for something is so strong that it blazes within the heart and mind at nearly all hours, it seems that people will put aside their fears, limitations and doubts. It is at this moment that we can connect and begin again.

"But, realize that, since most people think of their limitations often, it takes a tremendously strong desire to force one to act in faith. Really, this process should not be difficult, but fear and divided thinking are so prevalent in this world."

The caller spoke with reason, yet, in my own experience, I knew that I also greatly hungered for food, warmth and shelter. Clearly, I had a strong desire for such things, yet, in these times, they always escaped my gasp. I suspected that, if its words were true, I should have abundant meals, a warm cot and a sturdy loft to shield me from the cold. Once more, the caller's words did not match my experience of the world around me, and my doubt grew. The carriage stopped and amidst the jolt I clamored,

**"S-sir", why have we stopped here at this place?"**

"You will not see the true world around you, until you are ready. You will not understand the things that I will show you, until you accept the truths that create them. We must wait here until you are ready."

Just then, another question flashed in my mind, **"Sir, I know many who have desires for happiness, prosperity or even simple warmth and shelter. They greatly long for such things, but never obtain them. I also want these things. What of us?"**

"Do not confuse someone's immediate needs for true desire. Everyone wants happiness, food and shelter. Yet, immediate need, by itself, does not result in lasting creation.

"If you act only out of need, you will move only as far as it takes to end your pain or discomfort, or to satisfy this immediate need. Do you know someone who searches for food with vigor and then returns to idleness and laziness once their belly is full? When you act based on immediate need, you may be content with whatever random object, circumstance or person that comes your way."

The caller continued, "But when you are moved by true desire, you are moved by the higher self, by me. It is this true desire that urges you to seek the things held dearly in your heart. It is only this immense desire which will compel you to seize your inner power, release your dependence on the ego, and, with this new amazing self, create the world you seek."

Just as soon as my excitement grew, I could not help but think of my empty stomach and deep fears. **"Yet, how can I have** this grand desire when, at this moment, I need shelter and food?" I asked.

"Learn this Secret of the Ages," the caller whispered. "When you act to make your desires a reality, your immediate needs shall always be met. Yet, whenever you act only to satisfy your immediate needs, you will find only temporary satisfaction and frequent misdirection. In a short span of time, the person acting out of immediate need encounters the same lack, again and again."

Once more, I heard a tight crack of the reigns, and the cadence of the horse's hooves. I felt the rhythmic rattle and rock of the carriage car, and knew we were moving again. We soon came upon a merchant district, and here we saw a bustle of activity. The caller seemed unaffected by the noise and movement around us, and the carriage pressed onward.

**"Yet, Sir, I do not understand how this process shall enable me to obtain the outcome I want."** I persisted.

"There are desires that you have in your heart. *There are things that you once dreamed of but now you have forgotten. They are only faded memories buried deep within you* because you have convinced yourself that they are impossible to obtain.

"Go back to each and concentrate upon them. *You know exactly what they are.* Bring them into your mind, again and again. Hold a particular overwhelming desire for them in your mind, at all times. Create a picture of what you desire, and feel yourself obtaining it. As you go about your day tomorrow, bask in the glory of this future accomplishment; feel as if you have already claimed this prize. Then continue to act and move forward."

I began to shake my head. All of this seemed so impossible to accept. I determined that I must have proof and, so, responded boldly, **"But what mechanisms cause all this to be so?"**

"Thoughts, pictures and feelings held and repeated in the mind create patterns of thought and ironclad beliefs. Once these patterns and beliefs become fixed in your automatic or subconscious mind, they will propel you to immeasurable heights, or hurl you down toward your decline and destruction. Once you accept this as true, you will realize this law has always been at work in your life and all around you."

At that moment, a man crossed our path. He had freshly-ripped, brown pants, a curved, sloping posture and a shirt that looked as if it was trying to escape the very body it clothed. Everything about him seemed to be unmatched, disorderly and in chaos. In addition to his disheveled and slovenly appearance, he walked erratically. He crossed the street back and forth, and made great circles with each passing. Although I could see no impediments in his path or around his limbs, it looked as if, with each step, he was fighting the very air around him. I am sure you can imagine him, as well, if you try. As the man passed, the caller glanced toward me and then again at the man, as if to ensure my attention was placed on our disheveled new guest.

"This man longs for opportunity, much like you. He has traveled from a far-away city to search for opportunity. He has used all of this physical force to find it. Yet, just as it eluded him in his own town, it shall also elude him here.

"You see, this man's mind is detached from its true source. It is polluted with ideas of limitation and disorder. This man reads the daily papers that talk of political turmoil, dwindling resources, increased crime and other stories of decline. He continually laments his lack of education and his poor upbringing. *He lives in fear and in reaction to the world, instead of in faith as the creator of his world!*

"He has walked for miles and miles today, and has knocked on all doors seeking opportunity. All have been shut off to him. Do you know why?"

**"I do not know,"** I said.

"His progress is halted because of his limiting beliefs and what they have caused him to become. Before knocking on each door, he secretly curses each storekeeper. He re-lives the patterns of his past mistakes and he grumbles his circumstances as sure as each step is taken. The results of his physical efforts can never overcome the effects of his automatic or subconscious beliefs. As long as this man's mind believes in limited opportunity, failure and lack, his reasoning mind and confused eyes shall deliver to him an exact reflection of the same."

Frustration grew inside of me, and I blurted out, **"Yet this man is actively seeking, surely he must be rewarded!"**

"Remember, all people want better external circumstances, but very few will change their inner selves to obtain them."

The man continued about, and we slowly trailed behind any of his forward movements. Perhaps, I was the most troublesome of all people, yet, I did not understand how this man did not demonstrate true desire. Surely, the actions of his physical body were at least an inclination of his strong desire for opportunity. At the risk of appearing a meddlesome nuisance, I probed deeper:

**"Sir, please forgive me, as I do not want to be an annoyance, but it appears this man does desire opportunity."**

"Do not be fooled. An overwhelming desire can only exist when the mind believes that it can be made a reality. This man does not have such a belief.

"Other men with less skill have benefited the powerless, become captains of industry and humanitarians. Why is it that this man cannot even help himself? You see, he can never rise above his circumstance, until his inner beliefs change."

The caller paused for a moment, took its eyes off of our guest, and looked directly at me, "True desire can only exist when your mind absolutely believes that this desire will become reality. This is why a thousand footsteps and endless pleas for help can never permanently lift this man from his circumstance, or anyone else from their condition. Triumph can only come when your belief in the attainment of a goal is unquestionable and unrelenting."

I was as confused as perhaps anyone would be, and I cried out in aggravation, **"Why is this so perplexing? I do not understand how a man's footsteps and hopes could not be rewarded!**

The caller replied blankly, "These processes do not think in terms of arbitrary rewards. It is a case of cause and effect; it is an operation of law. Your mind is forever trying to match your internal world with your external world. In other words, it will deliver to you a reality comprised of your internal dialog and deep beliefs. If all of this seems confusing to you, it is because your conscious mind has not accepted it yet, and your ego fights it."

**"Sir, do tell me more,"** I pleaded.

The caller's eyes began to blaze brightly, "Everyone lives in a separate reality. It is a world created by each person's beliefs and by their perceptions."

**"But how may this phenomenon be possible? How can the mind change reality?"** I begged.

"It is really quite simple." The caller answered, "Imagine someone who believes the world is filled only with limitation and anger. Since the mind always works to equalize internal beliefs with external reality, this person's mind soon only will notice things in their surroundings that reinforce ideas of limitation and hatred. And, very soon thereafter, such a world is created all around them. The same is true for the person who truly believes in abundance, love and goodness."

We followed the disheveled man for some time, and I studied him closely. At the edge of the market, the disheveled man stopped at a dry goods store. Several oil lamps were burning in the store, and it was clear that someone was working late. The disheveled man stood peering into the window and basking in the golden hue of the lit shop. Inside the store was a neatly-dressed storekeeper who wore a bow tie. The storekeeper then glanced through the window at the man who was gazing inside. Both men seemed to connect with their eyes and, for a time, locked on to one another. The neat storekeeper then began to walk toward the door of his store.

Within a moment, the door of the store had opened, and the keeper was under the stoop at the entryway. Suddenly, a loud bellow came from the disheveled man's jaws.

"Y-yer lucky to have that store, but you don't wish to help a starving man! Yer a filthy cheat!" he barked.

Then, the disheveled man frantically motioned his knuckles in the air as if he was batting away a horde of invisible flies that swarmed around his face. He then gritted his teeth and began to growl. He stomped in the muddy puddles which lined the curbs, and splashes of water jumped and sprayed all around him. I had seen many rabid dogs growl, eat at their own hide and act quite oddly, as a young child. His actions seemed strikingly similar and alarming.

Then the disheveled man yelled, "To the hell fires with all of you!" and he stormed off.

My mind was reeling. I could not fathom the events I had just witnessed. Perhaps, most confusing, was that his actions seemed familiar to some of my own. Pleading for answers, I asked:

**"S-sir, these men knew each other, correct?"**

"No, they did not."

**"W-why then did the shopkeeper come to the door?"**

"The shopkeeper was amazed that, at the very moment he desired assistance, a man appeared in the window." The caller paused, and then added, "He was ready to pay good wages for help at this late hour."

**"Is this why they both seemed to gaze at each other for such an extended time? Please tell me S-sir!"** I pleaded nervously.

The caller seemed unmoved by my impatience and spoke slowly, "Both men's level of thought connected for a time. The disheveled man sought pay for any labor he could find, and the storekeeper realized he would need an extra hand to complete his re-stocking by dawn. Each man was united in thought, for a time. Amidst this short union, an opportunity arose. Yet, the disheveled man committed an act that many fall victim to."

**"What is that?"**

"He paid attention to his fear," the caller said sternly. "He paid attention to his destructive self. He relived the moment in which other shopkeepers told him they were not interested in his services.   He recounted this flash of fear and the pattern of disappointment until the same result was created once more."

I sat bewildered, and my eyes trailed downward toward a muddy puddle lapping at the curb below.

The caller continued, "You see, William, those who live in fear place all of their attention on such fear.  Each person's fears are different but, really, they are all quite similar.  As a result, they cut off opportunity.   They cut off their connection with me, their creative self.  They solidify a negative pattern, or map in their mind, and a set of limiting beliefs.  And their consciousness works to create and bring them the same outcome, over and over again.  This is how you may become captive to your fears."

I continued, **"Sir, what if a good pattern is held in the mind?"**

"Certainly, the law works indifferently," it said.   The caller's tone was quite heartfelt, and I sensed that it had a tremendous desire to reach me.  "Don't forget that, if you hold a belief about yourself or the world around you, your mind will work vigorously to transform or transmute this into reality.  It makes no difference if the belief is creative or destructive, positive or negative, empowering or limiting."

The caller then looked at me with radiating eyes, "In this manner, the mind may become one's liberator or one's iron-fisted destroyer.   Certainly, you have known people who, indeed, are their own worst enemy."

It was true. I did know of such people and, perhaps, you do as well.  I reflected on the caller's words for a moment and then, from somewhere, this question came, **"Could it be that what I concentrate upon affects my future?"**

"It creates your future! Remember, where you place your concentration, you place your vast creative power. It is because of this vast power that everyone is given unchallengeable and complete control over the thoughts they consider. Surely, you know that, as you deeply believe, you shall create and become."

**"Yes, it does appear so."** I said, rubbing my chin. **"So then it is my duty to watch over my thoughts and beliefs, Sir?"**

The caller smiled and then laughed, heartily. As it chuckled, it said, "Of course, it is! Could anyone else on this planet do this for you?"

The caller became serious and elaborated further, "The battle for control of your mind shall always begin by removing limiting beliefs about yourself and the world you live in. Then, you must guard your thoughts. You must stand as a watchman at the doorway, as a guard and protector of your thoughts and beliefs. Like a farmer, you must plant the correct thought seeds in the garden of your mind. Most people are unhappy because they have cut themselves off from their true self. This separation occurred because they failed to plant the correct thought seeds in their mind. Or, in many instances, they let someone else plant these seeds for them."

**"Are you saying that most people do not follow this approach?"**

"Certainly I am!" the caller said loudly. The caller then pointed to the area where the disheveled man was once standing and said, "Most people devote little time to guarding their thoughts. Their ideas, whims and wants drift with the conditions of life or according to what people tell them. As a result, their minds are generally filled with contradictions, limiting beliefs, and half truths."

The caller's tone then became stern and uncompromising. It looked at me with piercing eyes and unbridled power, *"You are absolutely unique and here for a special reason.* Yet, you may live and think according to what others do, how others reason, or based upon what foolish people have told you. You may re-live past hardships and disappointments each day, week, month and year.

"All of this creates fear in you. It is a fear that always lingers, but seems impossible to find. This persistent pain is called *doubt*. And for you to create anything you desire from life and to experience true joy, this doubt must be removed. The subconscious power of your mind must be focused upon your overwhelming desires and the absolute belief that only you can obtain them. This is how you were designed to operate. Anything otherwise is an abomination."

Never before had I heard such things mouthed with such clarity. It seemed that a part of the world was becoming simpler, yet these new ideas seemed so complex and daunting. I listened quietly, and desperately pursued each word with my intense concentration.

"When your subconscious and conscious mind become focused and directed toward a clear purpose, you will be propelled to move in this direction, at all hours. In this manner, your sight, your hearing and your perception are continually directed to seek out opportunities, people and situations that align with this definite purpose. You will also emit thought waves and impulses that connect with people, resources, and opportunities in alignment with your purpose. The very fabric of all matter around you can, definitely, be shaped toward creating what you desire in life.

"Do you wonder why some people seize opportunities to which others are blind? It is because these people act upon the creative impulses fed to them by the subconscious mind and their higher self. In this way, their mind has become a tireless servant, and shall work, at all hours, to propel them to create, attract, and build the pictures held within it.

"Act in this manner, and limitations that once determined your boundaries will easily be cast aside, your thinking will expand all around you and an amazing power will come to your aid. You are *no longer the same, you are no longer ordinary*, for you are what you were truly designed to be. *You are connected to your true self.*"

I sat in awe, yet, at the same time, overwhelmed. I felt like a slow, wooden spool trying to wind up copious amounts of incoming yarn. My body was still, but my brain reeled.

The night air was now quite tolerable, albeit chilly. I felt the carriage begin moving once more, and heard its creaking wheels pressing upon the ground as they rolled along our path. As the large wheels spun through the city, I looked down at the passing road below. A thick layer of mud now lay atop the street bricks, and a dark mist seemed to linger in the shadows. Slowly, I began to understand more and more of the caller's wisdom, but I could not be prepared for what I would learn next.

# CHAPTER EIGHTEEN

# Do You Know the Law of Polarity?

As the carriage continued to travel along the streets of Norfolk, we began to enter a district that I knew very well. The broad, mud-caked streets and trench-lined curbs were familiar to me. A wide expanse of darkness surrounded a large building that was lit by a single, dull lamp on a crooked pole. Alongside this building were tall pilings of heavy timber and freshly-cut planks. Wood shavings littered the area, and the fresh smell of cut and splintered pine lingered in the damp night air. I inhaled the smell of the cut pine, but it only made me cringe. This was the carpentry shop where I worked for a brief time, as a day laborer, after my dismissal from Wells Company.

A feeling of resentment, peppered with anger, came over me, as I remembered my time here. No one wants to recount bad experiences, and I was certainly no different. I desperately wanted to go somewhere else, and soon began to bark this wish at the caller.

"Sir, I don't want to visit this place! My destructive path began here. My petty work as a day laborer and the slurs from others in this shop could only cause me to slip further into hopelessness."

In a composed and serene tone, the caller responded, "A person's destructive path can never begin in a physical place. You were well on your way, when you accepted negative thought seeds and acted upon them. Your challenging experiences here were only the fruit of a seed you had already planted."

"You make it appear as if my thoughts produced this. This talk of fruit and seeds perhaps is impossible," I scoffed back, hastily.

Again, the caller was unmoved, and continued, "Although it may seem impossible to those who are ignorant of these laws, it is completely logical for those who understand them. An entire lifetime will unfold and develop around your accepted beliefs. A repeated thought becomes a belief. If this belief takes root in your deep subconscious, your mind will busily work to create a reality that mirrors these beliefs. While you may try to change day-to-day thoughts, any rooted beliefs will always bring you back to where you are now."

I tried to reflect on the caller's words, but my insides seemed to burn with resentment. It seemed so effortless to speak of different outcomes while sitting atop this carriage. As the memories of my decline clawed at my insides, I shouted back at the caller, gnashing my teeth after every other word or so.

"I had no other option! The unfair situation left me no choice!"

The caller persisted, "Make no mistake, all people may contemplate negative thoughts, at times. When things did not go your way, you had reason to be confused, upset, and even angry. But you have chosen to hold these negative feelings in a certain part of you. And this part of you continues to feed your mind thoughts of failure, hopelessness, ingratitude and contempt."

Angrily, I shot back, **"I met with great hardship. I had no other option but to travel down the path I took!"**

"True, you met with hardship, but choices were all around you. No matter the circumstance, all persons are free to utilize their own patterns of thought. In doing so, a man or woman first creates the future they desire within the mind. If this picture is held, repeated and acted upon, a pattern is created. Then, it will, undoubtedly, appear in the world around them. This cannot fail, for it is as inevitable as night and day!"

**"Sir, I wish to leave this place now!"** I angrily protested, with a fierce scowl.

The caller sat undisturbed. It seemed as if it was waiting for something, although I could not discern what. Just as soon as I had finished this thought, a small lamp began to glow in a back window of the upstairs office. Behind a dusty glass pane, I saw old man Hiedwig, the shop owner. I also noticed various coins and currency strewn across a table. He was smiling, as he counted the coins and stacked the paper bills into a tidy pile.

The sight sickened me. I assumed that the caller did not understand what was transpiring, so I sought to inform it.

**"That is Mr. Hiedwig, the owner of the shop,"** I said, with disgust. **"At this late hour, he is probably contriving more abundant ways to cheat and bleed his workers."**

The caller sat unaffected by my words, "William, do not live as a liar. Look closely into the window. Look beyond your clouded perception. You will see more."

As I looked again at the window, the outline of another figure began to take shape. I kept my eyes on the figure for a time, and then I felt shock, and some disbelief, as I realized that the second person was, unquestionably, a young man by the name of Jenkins.

**"What could he be doing in the shop at this late hour? This young man was a day laborer who had started work some time after me. He had very little experience and was quite unpracticed!"** I exclaimed.

"William, the young Jenkins is a manager now. He now assists Hiedwig in many matters of the shop."

**"A manager!"** I snarled.

Grumbling below my breath, I added, **"Certainly, they are partners in their efforts to cheat and beguile workers."**

"That is not reality, William!" the caller interjected. "Tonight, these men are counting up collections and donations for the family of a shop worker. You see, one of the workers has a very sick child."

Soon, another feeling overtook me, as I thought of the carpentry shop and Mr. Hiedwig. I recounted times when I had stolen tools and articles from Hiedwig, and delighted in these acts. It seemed that, at every turn, another world was being thrust upon me. Angry and frustrated, I stomped the floorboard of the carriage and moaned:

**"Why did the world trick me so? How could I have felt comfort from such acts, if he was trying to help his workers?"**

"William, you tricked yourself, just as most people do. You believed Hiedwig was effortlessly prospering while you were deteriorating. Of course, you never saw his late hours, his hard work or his acts of charity. You believed that Hiedwig, and all employers, only want to cheat their workers. As a result, you conditioned your mind to find and arrange facts so as to support these beliefs."

Shaking my head, I said, **"It seems impossible that such things occurred based on my beliefs. Perhaps, it was not my fault, but merely fate?"**

"William, understand the law of cause and effect! You believed that Hiedwig was paying you too low a wage and wanted to cheat you. As such, you thought your only option was to equalize this difference by theft. You never realized that Hiedwig was the first employer in Norfolk to trust you, after your dismissal from Wells Company and the public scandal. Hiedwig had faith, and he believed in you. In fact, the young Jenkins now occupies the position originally reserved for you."

With this revelation, a new pain pulled at my heart. I then demanded, **"Sir, this cannot be so!"**

"Indeed, it is not so any longer. You never came close to meeting Hiedwig's expectations. Yet, for a time, when you approached his shop years ago, he believed that you were honest. Honest, despite all the rumors and scandal circulating about you. He believed that, since you had managed some of Mr. Well's ventures, you would be a tremendous asset to his growing carpentry shop."

**"But, how could I have made such a grave error?"**

"William, remember the laws! Most people think they see the entire world around them, but each is living in a narrow reality created by their own beliefs. Each person's beliefs will slowly mold their life experience. In your situation, you began to think that the whole world was against you. You began to think that life was unfair. By accepting these thoughts continuously, they slowly became your beliefs. Soon, you were a loyal slave to your lesser self, your weakened form. As you accepted more of these beliefs, your mind noticed only things around you that maintained these beliefs. Your perceptions became altered, and your mind created even more thoughts to support them. In effect, you closed yourself off from all other possibilities."

**"I am sorry"** slowly seeped from my lips, and I had nothing more to say and no position to defend. I hung my head down.

Immediately I heard a snap of the reins and we were moving again. The carriage made a tight half-loop along the mud-caked road and we doubled back along our path. The motion of the carriage seemed to stir my spirits once more, and I asked:

**"Sir, where are we heading now?"**

"There is no destination, only a journey. I could take you anywhere in the city and show you the same truths over and over again. In reality, these laws surround you and surround all people at all times. Once you accept and understand them, they will prove themselves as true, all around you."

The slow rocking of the carriage and the plodding of our horse along its path seemed to bring forth an endless set of new questions. I still could not understand how I was so misled. It seemed quite strange that Mr. Hiedwig gave me an opportunity, yet, I believed that he wanted only to exploit me. How did Jenkins rise up through the ranks so quickly? So many questions seemed to float about my mind that I could only resolve to keep seeking answers.

**"Sir, how could I have been blind to all of these truths?"**

With its eyes on the road ahead, the caller explained, "You can have anything in life you truly desire, if you keep your thoughts and actions concentrated on what you truly want. Yet, your focus has been on all you do not want.

"You see, rather than rejecting the thoughts and beliefs which caused your fear, doubt and weakness, you continued to give your time and attention to them. In doing so, your false self became your dominant person. Your mind worked constantly to feed you with suggestions, create thoughts, and seek out situations, memories and people to prove that your new destructive beliefs were real."

The caller's voice grew loud and deep. It looked at me intently. "Do you not realize that your mind, at this very moment, is the vast storehouse of all your knowledge, and all of your positive and negative memories? Each can, easily, be brought forward to justify a current belief. If you believe there is no opportunity, then your mind will use its vast storehouse of information to prove this to you."

I reeled in astonishment. Just as you might, I found it disturbing, to imagine that my own mind would work against me. Fragments of ideas floated in and out of my head, until I uttered, **"Yet, how is it possible that I could be so deceived, so confused?"**

"Easily, if a ship has an ineffective captain, is it possible for it to run aground? Is it, then, possible for countless crew members to perish? Your mind is your captain. Consider how many rulers throughout history have destroyed the lives of thousands, based upon the inaccurate use of their minds? The mind is the captain of your body, and the ruler of your earthly experience."

**"How could my own mind trick me like this? How is it possible?"**

"Understand that when your mind becomes convinced of a negative or destructive belief, it will begin to assemble all known facts and even some contrived facts. All of these will be arranged to justify a current belief."

**"Is this what happened to me?"** I asked.

"Yes, William, this was your trap. You see, the mind can also manipulate your perceptions. It will cause you to notice things, people, and situations in your surroundings that mirror and support your current beliefs. These powers are so great that you became willing to live and die in a false reality, a fabrication. If you had charged your mind with creative beliefs, it would have sprung to action to uplift you. Yet, you fed it destructive thought and orchestrated your own demise."

The caller's presence was now uncompromising, and its countenance became as unyielding as heavy iron, "Grasp what nearly all people fail to learn during their entire lives: Both the destructive entity and creative entity share the same powerful secret. Then, it leaned over and whispered in my ear, *"Their dominating and never ending goal is supremacy!"*

Chills of cold ran up my spine and my skin turned to gooseflesh. It was the first time in my life that I had ever heard this word mouthed, although, somehow, I understood its meaning. To me, it was a word that carried great weight and severity. I could not imagine that each entity or self fought for power over me.

**"But Sir, how could the destructive entity want domination when you say that it would destroy me? Would it not destroy itself, as well?"**

"Indeed, you are slowly rising up from your sleep. The destructive self will, indeed, destroy you, and, in doing so, it is completing its purpose and attaining its highest ideal. This is its plan, its objective and its only aim."

All of this seemed too fantastic a proposition to accept. I thought that I had misunderstood the caller, so I asked for clarification, **"Did you say the destructive self seeks to destroy me? Why would it do such a thing?"**

The caller's presence became as unyielding as an imposing mountain, "Yes, and William, it is not a question of why, as these forces do not reason! Like matter can only produce like matter!"

The caller then stopped the carriage along the side of the road. What I heard next was a truth so ominous and frightening that still shudder today at the weight of these words. The caller continued,

"Now, please listen attentively!" the caller's eyes were now locked upon mine. These laws are absolute and immune from anyone's foolish haggling!

"Yet, in every century, you will find men and women who waste their entire lives trying to dicker and debate these rules. It is the primordial charade, the grand lie of humankind, and an age-old dark deception. The destructive force can only act to complete its purpose, to actualize its highest ideal.

"Like a tiny fly caught in a colossal invisible web, unseeing men and women will try to override these rules, but destruction for them is guaranteed. Service to the lesser self can only produce one result, one outcome and one fate: the absolute destruction of who you were meant to become!"

As the caller's words vibrated across the night air, the glowing carriage continued along its path. I clutched the caller's coat, in apprehension and anticipation of what might happen next.

# CHAPTER NINETEEN

# Do You Know the Great Lie?

A SMALL ORANGE SPECK DANCES ALONG THE water's edge. If you come closer, you may discern several darkened figures huddling and pacing about the orange flame of an open fire. Their bodies swarm by the glowing light, under a low bridge in the port district. As you move closer still, a large heavyset man with dark, brooding eyes and a large, gaping mouth is revealed. Two sparsely-built men concentrate on every word he speaks. It is clear that the heavyset man has their profound attention and is in control. When the heavyset man pounds his hulking hands together, the other men gasp uniformly, and then disperse a sinister chuckle into the heavy night air.

❧  ❧

FAR AWAY, AN OPEN, PHAETON CARRIAGE MEANDERS along the dark and narrow roads leading to the water's edge. The yellow light of the carriage lantern glimmers with its rocking cadence. The yellow light and the orange light seem destined to converge, but the carriage car stops 50 yards from the bridge.

**"Sir, why are we stopping at this point in the road?"**

"Can you see the orange fire burning under the bridge?"

**"Indeed, I do see it,"** I replied.

"What else do you see?"

I strained my eyes, and looked in the direction of the bridge and the bonfire. I could smell the familiar fragrance of an open fire, in the night air. I took a deep breath and enjoyed the smooth aroma of burning pine. I squinted my eyes and saw what appeared to be three men engaged in a very important discussion. A large man was talking loudly and pacing about the grounds. The pounding of his hands together usually caused the other men to flinch and jump for a bit, but, each time, they would lunge forward toward the large man again. The men seemed extremely focused on the subject matter of their discussion.

While the large man spoke and paced about, one of the other men was furiously scribbling into the ground, with a stick. If not for the strange location and circumstance of this meeting, one might assume that the large man was the executive of a large, industrial enterprise. The slight-framed men could well have been high-level managers. Their attention, focus and enthusiasm was impressive, albeit a bit odd.

**"I see three men engaged in very elaborate discussions, I think."**

"Indeed, you are correct. In fact, very elaborate plans for crimes and swindles," the caller revealed.

In a tone fitting a squeaking mouse, I whispered, **"Sir, are we safe here?"**

The caller laughed slightly, "Do not worry, these men's minds are so busily engaged in the creation of their plans, they have no interest in us or anything else around them."

I whispered, once more, **"Do you mean that they are contriving plans for criminal acts?"**

"Yes!" the caller exclaimed, "These cohorts spend their days scheming and creating plans for thefts and other unlawful activities. Pity them, for they do not understand the most fundamental truths of their own existence: The mind is constantly working to turn any accepted and repeated thought into reality. Most people never realize that their mind can work equally hard to create and build them, as it can to destroy them."

Again, I looked in the direction of the bridge and the bonfire. I thought of deliberations during my time as a manager with Wells Company. To be quite honest, these men may well have been discussing the expansion of industrial operations, the opening of a new saw mill, or even the latest scientific discovery. It is only if you crept closer that the dark motive behind their discussions would become very clear. At that moment, I came to realize the incredible power of thought. It seemed that thought and action could be used to propel a person to great heights of giving, achievement and joy, or wasted upon criminal acts and other foolish endeavors. At the moment of this revelation, the caller continued to explain these unfailing laws:

"William, do you realize that these men's minds could have easily used their force and influence to reach to the pinnacle of a desire or an ideal they chose to concentrate upon?"

I considered the question for a moment. Indeed, it did seem reasonable to believe these men could reach a high level of achievement, and I nodded my head.

"Yet, these men shall be an utter waste of human potential, and a cluster of fools. The prisons and institutions in all countries, territories and townships are teeming with those who are ignorant to this simple truth."

The caller paused for a moment and then said, "If you learn nothing else from this night, please remember what I am now about to tell you." The next words were quite shocking, and left me in awe of the truth being revealed to me:

"The minds of all men and women are never idle. Your conscious mind always searches for thoughts, ideas and circumstances to entertain and ponder. A great lie of the destructive self is that creative thought requires more effort. To the untrained mind, this may appear so, but it is a falsehood."

My eyes began to glaze over with confusion, and I began to shake my head nervously. It felt as if I was trying to grasp hold of air and miserably failing.

The caller recognized this, and said, "This is very important, so listen attentively! In your mind, there is no asking price for creative thought and no asking price for destructive thought. There never has been. *You may replace one with the other, at will.* In the mind, there is no greater cost, no greater effort and no greater distance to travel."

**"Are you saying that people can move toward their highest ideals, simply by choosing to focus and act upon them?"** I asked excitedly.

"Absolutely! In the mind, such a choice is effortless, but in the physical world, each choice will create an outcome. This outcome is the *greatest abyss known to humankind.* It is the difference between life and death, the difference between glowing success and miserable failure, the difference between health and utter sickness.

"A mere change of thought can hurl your life towards a positive or negative outcome. And this all-important choice is left to you, the individual. It is this consistent choice which will either put you in alignment with the forces that created the Universe, or absolutely against them. With no greater cost, effort, or distance, which do you choose?"

Looking out toward the bridge, I saw able minds churning out a plan that could only create more turmoil, loss and pain. Words and ideas circulated in my mind as I looked toward the men under the bridge, "A mere change of thought can hurl my life towards a positive or a negative outcome."

Indeed, we all have choices.

# CHAPTER TWENTY

# The Most Powerful Magnet

**W**ITH A PULL OF THE REINS, THE CARRIAGE NOW changed direction. The night was growing progressively clearer and I could see a faint twinkle of stars high up in the black sky. While the temperature was quite nippy, it seemed of less consequence now. The caller continued to address me, as the carriage wheeled toward the edge of the shipping district.

"Wise men and women throughout time have known the following rule to be true: Those with whom you associate will mold your thoughts and forge your beliefs. Yet, many falsely believe they are beyond these unyielding laws.

"Associate with people who dwell on thoughts of achievement, happiness, prosperity, and service to others and, alas, you will also rise almost effortlessly to such a level."

I tried to grasp the caller's words, but my concentration grew feeble and my mind began to drift once more. I started to gaze at the steady torrents of steam which were flowing from the horse's nostrils, and studied them. Each left a brief misty trail across the dark night air. I looked back and followed this long line of steam until I found myself staring at the budding stars.

The caller spoke once more, "The converse is equally true: If you associate with those whose thoughts are of selfishness, lack, fear and greed, these thought habits will slowly become yours, as well. Soon, you will begin to experience these miseries as your own!"

I continued to stare at the trail of vapor and the unfolding starlight. Then, unexpectedly, the carriage stopped and thrust me forward. In surprise, I turned my head toward the front of the car and was welcomed by a structure and place I knew well.

The caller then said, "Be warned, ignore this rule and this trap will ensnare you. Your demise may be swift or it may be gradual, yet, the destructive entity shall fulfill its purpose."

**"Sir, I remember this place,"** I said, and then chuckled softly beneath my breath.

"What can you tell me about it?" the caller asked.

**"It is a place where many people who have been let down by the world come to be at peace and to forget their troubles. I remember that, here, one could forget their pains, take life by the glass and dream of brighter days."** I smiled widely and eagerly, looking at it. **"May I have a visit?"**

"There is an old forgotten service door on the east side of this building," the caller said.

I wondered how the caller knew of any service doorway. I learned this place very well, but had never seen or heard of any such entrance. Nevertheless, I stepped down from the carriage and started walking.

I proceeded to the east side of the building in a careful, yet eager, fashion. I felt some joy, as I remembered how these grounds once eased my unrest. "Indeed, I should have come back to this place sooner," I thought to myself, as my steps hastened.

Imagine my surprise when, around the corner, a small crooked door hanging on old rusty hinges waited for me! I brushed off its soiled coating and pulled aside the brown vines that clung to its weather-worn exterior. I eagerly clutched its cold, green, brass handle. "Perhaps the visions of these sociable patrons will brighten my spirits," I thought to myself, as I pulled it ajar slightly. Immediately, I thrust my face in closer, to fill the breach.

A gust of truth, mixed with foul air, stung a blow to my eyes and nose. Through watery eyes, I saw a dim room with thick and noxious air, damp, muddy-colored walls and a low, black ceiling. The horrid smell of this chamber seemed to drip from its slimy walls. One breath would make most souls sickened and repulsed; yet, no one seemed to complain. There was one main doorway and no windows. The only light reluctantly crept from three faint, oil lamps. Each lamp emitted a deathly-yellow glow on the bodies swirling about this room.

It was a rum house, a liquor parlor, and, in the distance, I saw many of my past associates. Yet, I could never be prepared for what I would observe next. As the bodies danced and clamored about the room, I saw a suffocating grip upon them. I reeled in disbelief as ghostly-grey cords clasped tightly around their necks and about their heads. Each cord was clearly connected to a vaporous web which hovered in the center of the room.

As I looked deeper, I was horrified at the sight that came into focus. I realized that the grey cords resembled joints and bones. Like a long elastic skeleton, these unearthly cords glowed brightly against the dark walls and ceiling. A fog seemed to follow them and it created a cloud around their heads. Somehow, I knew that I was seeing the invisible form of hopelessness and gloom trapping them.

At that moment, I saw them as they were. I saw them as they tried to loosen the grip of emptiness, with unending quantities of drink, anger and disdain for those around them. While my eyes looked inside this rum house, I saw her now as a deceitful cheat. No longer, could her veil offer a disguise, and, tonight, her ghastly secret had been revealed. I wrenched and squirmed as the ethereal cords grew thicker, and the fog began to cover their whole bodies.

Emotion came over me like a heavy wave, pounding me senseless. "This place was none other than a self-imposed penitentiary," I whispered to myself. I began to feel wetness on my cheeks, and realized that I was sobbing. Indeed, I saw a cell packed with prisoners; fools left to grovel and claw in search of a false escape. Worst of all, I was once drawn by this illusion, as well. In the confusion and emotion of this whole experience, I began to cry more intensely. I quickly ran back to the carriage, in tears.

**"S-sir, what am I seeing? This is so repulsive to me now, how did it provide me with comfort?"** As I released these words, it felt like the weight of the world lay on my back. I rested my head on the carriage seat and began rubbing my wet eyes.

"You are seeing a secret world, William. This place and its people once provided you with a temporary illusion of relief."

**"How could I have been so mesmerized by this place and its people?"**

"William, you enjoyed their company because they made you feel better about your unhappiness. You felt better because your plight at the time was not as severe as theirs. So, they offered you a brief reprieve from your creative impulses to expand and to grow. For this temporary illusion of comfort, you bargained away very much.

"Many people fall into this trap and, indeed, it is no bargain. Soon, everyone's life will become similar or worse than the crowd they assemble with. From humankind's beginnings, this hollow swindle has trapped countless men and women."

While sniffling and wiping my eyes, I asked, **"B-but, I still do not understand why I sought out such a group and place like this?"**

"William, I shall demonstrate. After your dismissal from Wells Company, theft and hopelessness became part of your dominating thought and action. These thoughts and actions did not match your previous beliefs or the instinctive pulses from me, your higher self. As a result, thievery and hopelessness, for a brief time, brought you discomfort, pain and unhappiness.

"Such pain may have changed the course of your life and caused you to seek me once more. Yet, you ignored it and continued such actions. Soon, you became numb to these feelings.

"You became numb because your destructive entity took hold of your thoughts and altered your perception. As such, you believed that your pain was caused from circumstances created by others, rather than your own improper thought.

"Since you did not reject improper thought, the destructive force obtained further mastery over you. It called your attention to circumstances and to people in alignment with your new negative thinking. By seeking out all others who served their lesser selves, you became less likely to challenge these new beliefs."

The caller's words were absolutely true. It was, indeed, in this place and in this company that I fell to an even deeper low. It seemed that, with this crowd, I had little urge to do anything with myself and my dreams.  Some may think that this would be unpleasant, but, as you can imagine, it felt almost normal for a time.  How deceiving it all was.

It was so strange because, while I seemed to have control of my thoughts, their thinking was so pervasive that it tangled and intertwined with my own.  It was almost impossible to know where their thoughts ended and where mine began.

Still another question burned in my mind, **"Sir, why were these unfortunate individuals so plentiful?  Why did such persons continually come into my presence and I into theirs?"**

"Indeed, your lesser self arranged your mind's perceptions to notice only individuals with like thoughts and beliefs.  Similarly, these new associates were also drawn to you by the same such phenomenon, orchestrated by their own lesser selves."

**"How could all of us be drawn together, based upon thoughts?"**

"Indeed, all these men and women were emitting thought vibrations or impulses similar or equal to yours.  As a result, you tuned into their level of thought vibration and they tuned into yours.

Like a magnet, the level of thought one entertains will draw to him or to her people, things and circumstances which correspond exactly to such thoughts.  You were magnetized to them and they were magnetized to you.  Soon, you found yourself in places, situations and environments where similar thinkers resided."

**"Could correct thinking also draw to me beneficial ideas, impulses and opportunities, just as easily as it could attract defeat and lost opportunity?"**

"Absolutely, this is the precise reason why a person who maintains a consciousness of well being, no matter the temporary defeat, always rises back up. You will also understand why the person who has an inner consciousness of failure can only experience repeated failure.

"Can you now understand why men and women should always monitor their associates? An undeniable truth is that multiple minds directed toward a similar belief or purpose will propel you upward or downward with even greater swiftness and force. When multiple minds are directed towards one purpose, ideal, or belief, it is perhaps the most powerful magnet of all."

The caller's words, indeed, were all truth, but, according to my recollections, a small number of these people were kind-hearted and had good souls. Indeed, they were honest and caring, but had somehow lost their way. It seemed unfair to disregard them, so I interjected,

**"But, Sir, some of these men and women had quite unfortunate incidents in their days. Of course, many were contemptible and rancorous, yet, others were good and kind individuals."**

"It makes no matter. Such individuals will propel you downward in one form or another, because they are operating against the most powerful laws of the Universe. No matter their intent or goodwill, they will never overcome their circumstance until they prevail over their own habits of thought, and until they act and move from impulses of their higher selves.

"Mark these words well: Regardless of one's good nature or unfortunate circumstance, one who continually dwells on an unfortunate incident, painful memories or limitation can only remain a prisoner trapped in a self-created jail.

"Such people may wish, hope, or even weep for a better life, but, until they change their inner self, they can only remain a slave to a master, which yearns only to destroy them. Do you understand?"

**"Yes, I am trying, Sir, but tell me why these individuals must meet with continual pain, failure and loss?"**

"This reality exists because these misguided people are led by the destructive entity in some capacity. They do not realize that all successful and content people undergo struggles, loss and suffering.

"Regardless of the failure or physical incapacity, the individual guided by their higher self will always ascend to greater joy and understanding. This individual takes heed of any failure and torment as a priceless lesson. The path of this individual may change, as may her specific goals and aims, yet the lessons learned in failure shall propel her onward to greater and greater success and fulfillment."

The caller paused and then looked at me intently. As this might signal an important message, I concentrated deeply on what it said next:

"Never forget that when you continue to follow your higher self, no matter the failure, another route will always appear! Consequently, you will always find a more abundant opportunity, a deeper love, and a grander life. This is an unchallengeable law! "

At that moment, it seemed to me that failure might not be an absolute end, but only a signal. Immediately, my thoughts became words and I exclaimed, **"So failure might provide each person with a message?"**

The caller nodded with a slow and full articulation of its head. Its finger was now pointing upward and it added,

"Suffering and failure are the only means of growth for a person. If properly understood, suffering and failure allow for the removal of bad habits, improper thoughts, and weaknesses.

"The individual guided by the higher self will recognize that suffering and failure are not 'curses from God' or a 'downturn of luck.' These circumstances are an opportunity to learn and are the only means by which improper thoughts and action may be corrected. Failure allows proper thought and action to be strengthened in preparation for the greater victory and the greater happiness which lie ahead."

When the caller spoke of greater victory and happiness, it seemed impossible not to think of my own disappointments. Indeed, I had little excitement and no happiness to spring me from these sad times. I felt like my heart had fallen into a dark, bottomless well, so I cried out:

**"Sir, help me! I no longer feel happiness from this life!"**

"William, do not be sad! Your sadness is as understandable and as predictable as mathematics or the laws of the physical sciences. Stop your worries!

"Let me explain a Secret of the Ages: Service to the destructive entity will lure many to seek short-lived pleasures, such as unearned compensation, excessive drink, wickedness, laziness, fraud and games of chance. No matter how many of these activities a man or a woman partakes, they will only feel a deeper emptiness. Yet, like fools in a spiral of death, they will also seek more of the same.

"Always remember that these activities can never satisfy your deepest need for growth and service; the true reasons you are here. Did you not find that you were left with an even greater emptiness, regardless of how many of these activities you undertook?"

I thought for a moment and so it seemed that little by little, wrong thinking, theft, drinking and sloth eroded away my very core. In the end, I felt as if I were diminishing and becoming hollowed and more vacant with each passing day. Within less than a year, it seemed that I had become an unfilled casing, an empty vessel, a void and vacant shell. I responded with certainty:

**"Yes, it's true more and more of me became lost as time went on. Is this because of these rules?"**

"Well, of course! The same cause can only produce the same effect. If you operate against all elements of natural law, all elements of the laws must only work against you.

"Be wise and learn the truth at this moment: You are, by your very nature, a creative being! As a creative being, service to the destructive entity in any capacity will never result in lasting happiness, peace, prosperity, joy or good health."

When these last words were spoken the carriage began to stir and creak again. As we plodded along, I saw something from the corner of my eye that left me numb. Imagine my astonishment, as I witnessed the disheveled man from earlier in the night being drawn into the rum house. The out-of-town migrant was swept up by the hopeless mass, which wandered in and out of the tavern. Immediately, I turned around, climbed toward the rear of the carriage and reached for him. I, then, jumped from the carriage and tried to find him. Strangely, I was invisible to him. He had become one with the horde, and they had become one with him.

# CHAPTER TWENTY-ONE

# Are You the Jailor and the Prisoner?

"WHOM DO YOU BELIEVE TO BE THE CAUSE OF your present condition?"

I hesitated and then stumbled, **"S-sir, I c-cannot say."**

The caller pressed, "Whom do you believe to be the cause of your present condition?"

The heat of resentment burned in my gut, and now it flowed into my face. My cheeks grew warm, as I spoke, **"In truth, I still believe that I am a victim of the greedy heirs of Mr. Wells. They sought to remove me because I did not have the education, background and standing as they!"**

"You hand control over to your destructive self, yet you never question its command? You and you alone are the creator of your present condition. You are the jailer and the prisoner.

"Have you forgotten the circumstances surrounding your dismissal? Did you forget the power of your destructive self to warp perception?"

"Sir, I do not understand, for I was the victim of unfairness and bad luck."

"Circumstances do not create the person; rather, they expose his weaknesses and his improper thoughts. Remember that it was you who decided to expend the resources of the mill after the death of Mr. Wells. You obligated the mill to bank notes and additional loans, correct?"

My heart was now beating wildly, and it seemed that a tumultuous fire raged in my stomach and face burned red hot. As you can imagine, I felt like an animal trapped in a noose.

"It is true I did do this, but –" The caller took no amusement in my efforts to distort truth, and it interrupted,

"You did not consider the rising costs related of other business operations of the estate. These operations were strained by the death of Mr. Wells. Indeed, your mill was profitable, but you exceeded your authority and were blind to the overall financial situation."

The caller then whispered, "A competent manager would never have considered the operations of one venture as separate from the overall financial picture."

Trying to exert my own control, I responded in an ear-splitting yell, "Sir, I wanted only to show them that I could be effective in my post!"

The caller's voice remained calm yet stern, "Again, your understanding has been warped. You wanted to benefit yourself at the risk of the entire estate, did you not? Ask yourself, which entity did you serve?"

"I wanted to show them that I could run the business in a far superior manner." My anger began to increase.

"That feeling grows stronger now William, tell me who you served."

My hands began to vigorously pound against my knees, **"I do not know!"**

The caller's voice was stern, "I told you I cannot connect to the mind of one who thinks of defeat or failure and blames others for their situation. Ask yourself now, which self did you serve?"

The caller repeated its request, "Ask yourself who you served!"

My face grew white hot, and it felt as if a torrent of fire was rising from my belly. With these words I released it, **"I wanted to prove –"**

My feet began to stomp against the floorboard of the carriage car. I tried to hold my tongue still, but it was impossible, **"Prove myself superior to the entire lot of greedy, spoiled heirs. I had little and they always had everything. I was never good enough, too poor, with a father who left and even a mother who deserted me by death!"**

The caller paused for a moment and then looked at me, warmly, "Your actions had nothing to do with the heirs, but your own deep subconscious beliefs about yourself. William, the circumstances which affected you as a young child are still affecting you today. Your destructive self so clouded your mind that you took its counsel. Your actions had nothing to do with helping the business, but were only a response to your past life events."

The caller continued, and soon unveiled news that nearly leveled me, "This may not please you, William, but you should know the truth. The heirs of Mr. Wells were, in fact, very impressed with you. Your name was frequently discussed at meetings, events, and among shareholders. You were quickly rising, and the heirs were delighted with your performance."

**"Sir, it is not possible!"** Just then a pain most similar to what I felt outside Hiedwig's shop earlier this evening pounded in my chest and stung deep in my gut. With each word, the pain only intensified, **"I knew such heirs wanted my removal, because I clearly sensed it!"**

Again, I felt tricked, cheated, and misled. I had taken advice from the wrong counsel. Anger and sadness melted together into a weight called heavy despair. I felt dejected and demoralized.

"William, don't be angered. The past is no more. Remember this: A person will never learn the lessons from his failures unless he realizes that he and he alone is the cause of them."

**"Sir,"** I replied with my voice crackling, **"if I had realized these truths then I might have tried again. Yet, I felt so hopeless, and that my future was a random incident of chance. I decided, then, not to expend efforts as I once did."**

"Certainly, and by acting against these laws you caused the vast powers of the Universe to work against you. Never forget, a belief that life is random and hopeless is a trick of the destructive self. It is yet another age-old deception.

"Everyone will meet with suffering and disappointment, as all humans will; it is part of the plan. Yet, difficulty and failure are only temporary when you continue forward with proper thought."

**"Why, then, did I feel bitterness and contempt for the successful, the strong, for those in control?"**

"Remember, your mind will consistently work to create an external world that mirrors your beliefs. For example, you began to despise anyone who had what you wanted. For you to tolerate your newfound laziness, vagrancy and begging, your mind had to trick you. Your lesser self justified its existence by programming you that advancement and achievement were the result of 'luck' or cheating.

"At this point, you could only act against your true desires. In this way, you became the sole hand of the repressor and only creator of your torment in life.

"Mark these words well, William: Beliefs held in a particular manner, shall force you to live in a particular manner."

# CHAPTER TWENTY-TWO
## What Do You Hear?

AN ELEGANT RED AND BLUE SILK BANNER HUNG high on a lamppost at Church and Main Street. It was one of many which, traditionally, draped the city on New Year's Eve. The main section of the banner was spun from blue silk that looked as if it had been spooled for a king. It had an exquisite red border, with golden yarn that billowed into large, round and oval loops. A fluffy, silk edge outlined the blue center sections of the banner, and passersby said that it looked like a river of gold was flowing about its fringes. The maker of the banner originally planned to use gold only on the border sections, but, at the last minute, he, generously, decided to use the golden yarn to outline the important letters found in the center.

I learned, years later, that no banners were ever hung until the morning of December 31st. Yet, for some reason, which no one could explain, a single banner hung at the corner of Main and Church Street on the night of December 27, 1885. Attached high on a lamppost, the brilliant red, blue and gold banner danced in the wind.

FROM A DISTANCE, A PHAETON CARRIAGE WITH ITS single, flickering, yellow lantern, approached. As it neared Church Street, the important letters at the center of the banner caught the golden specs of light emitted by our lantern. As the carriage drew closer to the intersection, it looked as if golden butterflies were dancing around each letter. For a moment, the following words came to life: "NEW YEAR 1886."

The writings on the banner cried out to me, as our carriage wheeled past Church and Main that night. Amidst the gusts of wind and the lantern's glow, the golden numbers seemed to dance and sing before me. But, their songs were cries that warned of troubles, fears and uncertainty in the coming year.

I began to think of the men and women who accompanied me along my downward path. It seemed normal to hear of their stories of lack, inner turmoil and continual pain. I believed this to be the ordinary condition of all people in these times. Many of my associates claimed that these conditions would only continue to worsen with the passing of each year. The New Year, for most, meant lack, fear, and uncertainty.

I slowly addressed the caller, as these thoughts tumbled around in my mind, **"Sir, many of the men and women spoke of difficult times in all regions and that opportunities are fading. There was talk that the New Year would bring more unhappiness, greater ills, and increased uncertainty."**

The caller was booming in its response, "Irreverence and ignorance! Do not fear the coming year. Every day is a new year, every moment can be a new beginning."

"But Sir, they assured me that the years beyond 1890 would bring even less opportunity and the decline of humankind. Could this be true?" I asked.

"Do not accept any of these silly ramblings as truth. Similar unknowing people have uttered these cries since the beginning of all human history, and they will continue in the future!" the caller explained.

"These are fabrications of the destructive entity reverberated by the tongues of misguided men and women. Such people always believe that opportunity, health, fulfillment and peace are remnants of the past, and lost upon a new world."

I countered, frantically, "Yet, why would they make such claims, unless they had merit?  Certainly, my life has declined and many around me have suffered the same fate."

The caller answered, in an unaffected tone, "William, those who make these foolish claims do not understand the most basic workings of the Universe and the higher self."

"But, Sir" I whimpered, "The banner cried out to me songs of loss, lack and misfortune!  Should I expect it to lie, as well?"

The caller looked at me and said, "William, the songs you hear and the voices that sing to you are only a reflection of your inner beliefs, and messages from your destructive self."

The caller's expression then began to glisten and its eyes overflowed with promise, "You see, if one door is closed, the higher self, if fostered, *will always open two more*.

Do not believe that suffering and failures are permanent. Do not believe that opportunities are dwindling.  Do not believe that happiness, health and peace are fleeting."

"Sir, I do not understand, please tell me more."

"William, realize that, if a man or woman builds and fosters their creative self, alas, a better route appears, another great supply is found and more bountiful possibilities always surface. This is an inevitable law which always proves to be true! You will find that one who continually thinks of sickness can only attain more sickness. The wretched woman who complains of lack and suffering will only encounter more lack and suffering. The employer who continually believes he will lose his storefront will inevitably meet with such fate. Similarly, the person who complains that there is limited opportunity will meet with examples and demonstrations of this at every turn."

The caller then said, "If you examine your own self-created circumstance, you will find much similarity."

Still, I did not understand how two realities could exist at the same time, thus I probed deeper, **"How is it possible that two such realities or realms can exist at one time? How is it that on the same corner, one may find his death by lack while another finds plenty?"**

"You need only look to your own experience. Do you remember how, just before this journey, you were fearful, unhappy, and embracing things so unbecoming of your pure self? Can you now see the power of the destructive force in your own life and deeds?

"How can we occupy the same night air where you once fell among the cracks and begged for death; yet, now we enjoy a clear night and speak of strength, life and hope? Why do new ideas, beliefs and thoughts fill your mind with possibility and joy? You are being shown, without question that two realms do exist!

"The destructive self will thwart the eyes, ears and mind to only see and experience lack, fear, doubt, superstition, greed, jealousy and sickness. Whichever ill you choose, it will deliver."

The carriage then began a slow and steady incline. As the carriage gradually climbed, a shudder also climbed up my spine. I began to realize that two people could see and experience vastly different realities. I remember thinking of the word 'multiple' and that each person could bring into their reality the things and feelings they desired. Indeed, if each person created their own future by their thoughts and bodily actions, it also seemed that each person could exist in a different reality.

As the carriage neared the top of the hill, I quickly turned around as if someone had called my name from down below. At the bottom of the incline, I, again, saw the banner dancing in the wind, its fringes and lettering glimmering in the moonlight.

As I stared at it, I was immersed by this latest discovery. It was true that one could attach their own meaning to the events of life. And it was this precise meaning that set into motion another similar future event, occurrence, and perception. Over and over again, these meanings created each person's life experience. As I watched from a distance, the golden numbers and letters continued to dance and sing. Yet, now they sang a different tune, and I heard songs of excitement, certainty, and love.

# CHAPTER TWENTY-THREE
## *Your Connection*

B IT-BY-BIT, THE CARRIAGE JOURNEYED CLOSER TO the wharves. True, it was among the bustling activity of this area where I first found opportunity some years ago. But the place where I so proudly worked, now only brought me sadness. The hope I felt during those early days was a striking contrast to this murkiness. Determined to avoid more pain, I quickly spoke up.

"**Sir**" I said tugging at the coat of the caller, "**I do not wish to recount my time at the ports. I see only sadness here!**"

The caller did not respond to my pleadings, and the carriage continued along its route until it reached the berthing stations. With a loud 'creak,' it stopped, and, in an instant, the caller had stepped out and began walking.

"William, the hour is getting late and the journey beckons, be quick!"

"**Sir**" I cried out shaking my head, "**I do not wish to visit this place!**"

The caller responded, "William, I cannot reach the mind of one who thinks of defeat and who blames others for their situation."

I could only bumble and stutter a response, **"S-sir!"**

I realized that the caller spoke the truth. For this journey to continue, I also must continue. With this realization, I stepped down from the carriage and ambled towards the docks and shipping lanes. For the first time in many years, I walked the shipping lanes. As I stepped along the familiar berths and slips, memories of my early days in Norfolk flashed in and out my mind.

The chilly air blasting across the water and the familiar cry of the sea birds brought back many memories. It seemed that, upon my arrival in Virginia, I envisioned boundless opportunity. It seemed coincidental, but it was on that very day when I obtained a position at the docks. In those days, I had a belief that I could do anything I desired, and, lo, such belief became reality! I remember the compulsion to move, to act, and to proceed without delay. And it seemed like the world was waiting to give me what I asked for.

The caller was walking quickly ahead of me, but somehow I knew exactly where its steps would lead us.

**"S-sir, but, if one is surrounded by lack and poverty, how can they see opportunity?"**

"Understand this simple truth: Opportunity is all around you," the caller replied. "The Universe always creates an oversupply of opportunity. But, you can only see true opportunity when you serve the creative self. If you hear someone complain of lack and no opportunity, realize that the destructive self rules their existence.

"Remember, we will only see that which we project in our mental images; that which we truly believe to be true."

When these last words were spoken, the caller stopped and snapped its cane upon the ground. A loud 'crack' vibrated across the clear night air. The caller then raised one index finger and said:

"Mark these words well, because this is perhaps the strangest of all truths: While the creative force may allow you to see and discover opportunity, you must move quickly to seize it!"

**"Move quickly, Sir?"** I said, shaking my head. **"I am afraid that I do not understand."**

"You will understand, soon" the caller responded.

The caller sat on a tall barrel that had been perfectly positioned near the water's edge. I thought it peculiar that right along its side was another shorter barrel of less heft. Both directly faced the berth where I first began employment.

"William," instructed the caller, "please sit down here."

I slowly sat down on the barrel and reluctantly turned my head toward the familiar berth, quickly my eyes pointed downward. All I could see were my worn, ragged shoes and dirty legs. I so much wanted to ask the caller for permission to go back to the carriage. Yet, before I could utter another sound, the caller tapped its cane on the ground and then pointed it toward the familiar berthing station. I immediately looked up, and the caller asked:

"Do you remember this place?"

**"Y-yes, indeed I do,"** I said quietly. I had no desire to remember it, but it now seemed impossible to avoid. In a dejected tone, I continued, **"This is the place where I found opportunity... on the first day of my arrival."**

"Do you remember how you began your service here?"

**"I wish I could, Sir. Perchance, good luck was with me on that day."**

"Luck!" the caller exclaimed loudly, "luck is an imaginary idea, only a word clamored by fools to explain away the truths all around them!"

The caller continued, "You began service at these ports because you were guided by me. I am your higher self. You connected to my power because you directed your mind to a specific objective, and you had faith. In doing so, you were one with my force and one with all creative force. It is quite simple, but so many never learn this great truth. Do you recall how you felt that day?"

I thought back to the day of my arrival and it was clear that I urgently wanted to get involved. Perhaps, beyond this, I seemed to have a terrific desire to give service. I remember nearly overflowing with confidence and expecting only good.

**"I do remember how I felt."**

"Of course you do! Don't ever forget it! Do you remember that you saturated your mind, day and night, with the consuming desire of obtaining a position upon your arrival? Did you know that you engaged your automatic or subconscious mind, and it worked tirelessly to bring your ideals and desires into reality? Because you put aside all of your past rules about yourself and acted unselfishly, you could only connect to my power."

**"I never knew."**

"And it was my prompt and my command that instructed you to quickly proceed toward the docks. You were exuberant with joy that day, and the prospect of success loomed heavily. You were connected to my force, and because of this, you were connected to the force of all creative things in this Universe. It was as if everything aligned to meet the desires idealized in your mind; and if the truth be told, everything did so align.

You witnessed men unloading a small vessel, did you not?"

**"I did, Sir. Yet, how do you know all of this?"**

The caller paused for a moment and a wide smile beamed from its face.

"Earlier that morning, a woman wearing a bonnet called you a rapscallion, did she not?"

The caller then bellowed a loud rousing laugh that served as a compelling answer to the question posed, "Do you still believe your destructive self guided your steps?  Do you?"

A startling occurrence did then take place; as for the first time in years, I felt a smile crack the fixed scowl of my face. Although the air around me was quite brisk, warmth surrounded my body, and my chest felt full of pride.  The caller then continued:

"William, I brought the idea, the intuition to your conscious mind, and so propelled you to move. The true self of each person brings such urgings to aid them in their path.  Of course, many people choose to ignore intuition and remain asleep to the true miracles of life."

**"Yes"** I said in an excited clamor. **"Well, I do recall that men were unloading cargo.  In my mind, I clearly saw myself busily unloading the craft as well.  Almost unexpectedly, I climbed aboard and began passing grain bags to the men above. Peculiar as it seems now, I never held any fears or envisioned the possibility of refusal.  I just acted!"**

"Quite so, you seized the opportunity.  At the time, there was only one man on the small craft, do you remember this?"

**"Y-yes, I do remember this fact,"** I answered, quickly. My excitement was outpacing my words, and I began to become short of breath.

"Now, can you recall what happened next?"

**"Y-yes,"** I took a deep breath of air and continued, **"W-well, it was barely a minute that did pass and then two other**

men approached. They came from a building overlooking the wharves. One of these men was the berth manager. I don't know who the second man was, but he did communicate something in the ear of the berth manager."

"Indeed, the man who whispered into the ear of the manager was the owner of the vessel which you boarded. He commented on your swiftness, your spirit, your haste, for he was at one time a port laborer himself.

He also informed the port manager that it would be prudent to hire such a good worker."

"Yes, yes! But of course!" I said loudly. "Well, it was on that day when I was given a position. Oh, how my luck, my life did flow in such days!"

The caller looked at me and then stated blankly:

"Mark these words well: You earned the opportunity because you connected with me, your higher self. Unknowing people will tell you that your success was created by the laws of chance, the tides of favorable circumstance, or by sheer luck. These fools may never understand that each success is drawn to a person by consistent thoughts, consistent actions and preparation. An unprepared man who meets with opportunity only makes himself an embarrassment."

A strong twist of wind blew northward across the Elizabeth River and it quickly reached the area where we sat. My once scattered hair was pulled back against my scalp and I could feel sprays from the water touching and cleansing my skin.

"Do you still believe that a downturn of luck created your current state?" the caller asked.

The sound of the wind began to overwhelm my words. "I did once believe this!" I said loudly.

The wind gust had grown stronger and louder. Although the caller never changed its tone, each of its words could be heard clearly. "Never be foolish again," the caller said.

The coil of wind left us and, immediately, a temporary window in the cloud cover appeared. This window allowed the full radiance of the moon to shine down upon us and to sparkle atop the rippling waters.

**"I understand, Sir. But can you tell me why I moved with such haste toward the docks that day?"**

"Perhaps it is an unexplainable phenomenon, yet, the laws of success and happiness act against the lazy and uncertain. Opportunity does not wait for the slow, the idle, or the indolent. Windows of opportunity open and close quickly. Just as moving clouds can transform in shape and position, opportunity acts in much the same manner. You must always be prepared to act and move with faith."

Just then the temporary break in cloud cover closed off. I began to understand that windows of opportunity were similar to a cloudy sky, always opening and closing at various times. Yet, while the moon no longer shone down on us at this moment, I knew that it still existed. I knew, of course, that I would see it again, soon.

The caller then asked, "Do you recall a compulsion to act quickly?"

**"Yes, I remember that I had a desire to move with speed."**

The caller nodded its head and said, "Indeed, I knew that this particular opportunity had a limited window of time. So, I propelled you to move. Had you ignored my urge to seize the feed bags, do you know what would have happened?"

**"N-no, Sir, I do not know.  Please tell me!"**

"You would have been cast off the docks as a vagrant, a trespasser, a loiterer!  The berth manager would have removed you just as he walked from the offices.  Yet, you acted quickly."

The caller then looked at me with great enthusiasm, and said, "You are far enough along your journey to understand another vital truth about that day."

**"W-what is it, Sir?"** I asked gingerly.

"William, your actions not only benefited yourself, but changed the lives of many more that day, and beyond."

**"S-sir?"** I responded in astonishment, **"I am afraid that I do not understand."**

"I told you that you would learn a great many secrets on this night.  Are you ready to receive them?"

**"Y-yes"** I said, with my body twitching in a jumbled mass of excitement, wonder and optimism, **"I am ready."**

"Do you remember the moment you climbed aboard the docked vessel and began unloading it?"

**"Indeed, I do remember that moment, Sir."**

"The man who normally assisted with the unloading of that vessel was late for work that day.  In fact, he was no more than 100 feet from the docks at the moment your hands touched the first bag.  This man saw you working and was struck by your enthusiasm and your will.  For many years, this man had been considering another direction for his life.  In fact, he dreamed of being the captain of a ship.  When he saw your enthusiasm for his post, it was the final push.  It was a clear message for him to seek another trade.  Your actions propelled him to act and to move toward his higher purpose and listen to the urgings of his true self.

And, once this man connected to his purpose, he did, indeed, take over as captain of a merchant vessel."

**"Oh, Sir, I cannot imagine such things were set in motion because of me!"** I responded, with some disbelief.

"Do imagine and embrace these truths, because, in fact, there is much more to the story. As a result of his great skill in stormy and tempestuous seas one night, he was able to save the lives of all thirty of his crewmen. These men would have been lost at the hands of another captain.

"Indeed, William, it was his skill that saved their lives, but it was also his guidance that influenced them in many other profound ways. One of these crewmen recently became a father. One day his child will grow to become a great leader. This leader shall be very important to the future of many nations and shall also save countless lives. There are many more stories to tell and each is inexorably and inescapably connected to yours."

At that moment, I began to weep tears of relief and happiness. While I still did not understand how any waves of consequence could be set into motion by me, I still felt a deep peace. And, for the first time in my life, I realized that, no matter how alone I felt, I was linked to everything and everything was linked to me.

**"Sir, how is it that recently I have only been able to think of myself and my lowly conditions?"**

"You have been listening to your destructive self, your small ego, and it has tricked you into believing that your life has no significance. It causes all people to believe that they are alone and adrift on a meaningless and empty sea of chance. This is absolutely false. Do you remember the day you left New York for Virginia?"

**"Yes, I do recall that day."**

"A young boy named Phillip Dangle also lived homeless among other vagrants of the rail yards. Do you remember him?"

**"Indeed, I do remember a homeless child named Phillip. He was, perhaps, 5 years younger than me."**

"Yes, and Phillip watched while you labored for the storekeepers and merchants. He lurked around corners while you hauled carcasses, cleaned soap barrels, and hoisted debris.

"Your effort and labor kept his spirits flowing, and gave him hope. Yet, when young Phillip no longer saw you laboring for the shopkeepers, he fell back into despair. This child planned to step in front of a Washington Line rail car in July of 1873. It would have ended his life."

A flash of shock overtook me as I remembered that I had boarded a car on the Washington Line in the same month of that year. I blurted out:

**"Oh, Sir, I left on the Washington Line! I left New York in July of 1873!"**

"Indeed, you did, William. Thankfully, you followed through with your plan and this put an end to young Phillip's plan."

Puzzled and confused, I asked, **"Oh, please, Sir, how could I have ended his plans?"**

"Because, on the day of his scheduled suicide, he saw something amazing take place."

The caller leaned forward, and its bright face was no more than six inches from mine. Its features beamed and cast a warm glow into the opaque night air. The caller then whispered the following revelation to me:

"He saw you climb aboard the Washington Railcar Line."

A feeling of completeness and peace overtook my body and mind. I quickly broke into tears. I might say that, in places where I once suffered from hollowness, I now felt solid. It may appear strange to you, but something in my body rose up, and I remember feeling as if my essence flowed out in every direction, all around, above and below me. I felt a connection to everyone and everything. From the smallest particle and to the largest mountain, somehow, all was one. For the first time in my life, I felt an all-encompassing unity and joy. It was a profound sensation.

**"Oh, Sir,"** I said sniffling, **"Where is Phillip now? Is he safe?"**

"William, indeed, he is safe! And, one day, you shall see him again." The caller leaned in, once more, and then whispered,

"In fact, many people will see him, for he will occupy a very important public role in the next century!"

With its head back and voice commanding once more, the caller added,

"William, understand this fact: When you follow the creative self, it not only benefits you, but the world at large. Never forget that you are connected to a much larger web, and that your actions always impact the world around you.

"Following my instruction does not mean that you are seeking selfish ends, but it means that you are taking you own unique path. And your true path can only allow you to grow and be of greater service to all people. Like a stone dropped in a quiet pond, a ripple is created which impacts the lives of countless individuals."

At that moment, the moon once again shone down on the rolling waters. It appeared as if thousands of crystals were skipping across the top of each swell. I sat, contemplating these new revelations, for a time. I thought about how opportunity could show itself again and again to the person who served their creative self. I thought about how I was connected to everything. I thought about those now living, and even those who would come later. *I thought about how someone, perhaps not yet born, might even be connected to me.*

It, then, became clear that following true unselfish joy is not only our right, but our duty, because no one else will do it for us. I also recognized that duty and joy were one in the same, when you served the creative self.

I realized, at that moment, if one follows their true desires, it not only benefits their own purpose and plans, but others, as well. With these incredible revelations ablaze in my mind, my eyes opened wide and a smile stretched across my face.

**"Sir, Sir, so it is not selfish to follow my own desires, aims and dreams?"**

"Indeed, it is never selfish to follow your own true desires. They were put in your heart for the higher good. In fact, the failure to follow your creative self is not only foolhardy, but also is selfish and egotistical. When you follow your ideal purpose, you can only assist others along their own path."

"Remember this" said the caller, with one finger raised high, "the more you follow your true self, the easier it will be to understand and identify which self has compelled you to act. This is why those who seek me continue to find greater opportunity and happiness, and it is why they always impact the world around them in more significant ways."

**"Should move quickly when the creative self inspires me to act?"**

"Indeed, William, here is a fundamental rule which the wisest men and women always follow:

"When the creative force inspires you, do not fear! Move forward! Always act quickly, logically and respond to your instinct!

**"Sir, what if the destructive self calls?"**

"Alright" the caller smiled, and then paused for a moment, "please, grasp these next words securely, because there is another consideration: When inspired by the destructive force, do have disbelief. Wait to act, and always question its command!

"Can you calculate how many have destroyed their lives and the lives of others because they did not heed these two fundamental rules? How many rot in jail cells, or prematurely ended their lives and the lives of the innocent because they did not understand these unchanging truths?"

**"I cannot fathom the number, Sir."**

In short time, we were back in the carriage, though it seemed that we had just arrived at the port district. I realized that, in this span of time, I was discovering truths that may elude others for an entire lifetime.

# CHAPTER TWENTY-FOUR
# An Unstoppable Law

As THE REINS PATTED THE HORSE'S NECK, ITS familiar cadence reminded me that we were moving again. The carriage car shifted from side-to-side, as it meandered through the streets and thoroughfares of the city. Its wheels creaked and scraped as it rolled along the brick road. I watched the caller control the reins in its statuesque manner. Its face changed less frequently at this point in our travels, and for the rest of the night it maintained one countenance. As you, the reader, may wonder what I saw, I shall elaborate. Its face was of a man with strong and piercing eyes, deep and blue. It had golden brown locks flowing like a river under its hat, and a slight nose rested on a very pleasant visage. But, changing faces were of little interest to me now, because I now dwelled on its enduring and more meaningful wisdom. In truth, my curiosity also lay in the journey and where we would travel next. I continued,

**"Sir, where are we going now?"**

With its eyes firmly pressed on the road before us, the caller responded, "There is no destination, only a journey."

Slowly, I began to realize that, indeed, the lessons of this journey had proven more important than arriving at any one destination. I also believed that, if I could apply the knowledge of this night, I should find opportunity, once more. Yet, as soon as these thoughts entered my mind, a flash of fear arose from a deep place. I began to worry that, once a foothold of opportunity was seized, I might slip again and then quickly lose it. As the memory of past failures came upon me, my stomach burned, and it felt as if the chains of fright were pulling, again, at my internals. Immediately, the caller broke my specter of fear, with these words:

"Once you take hold of your objective, continue to think and act with the same haste and desire that led you to it. The first step to maintain success and growth is to continually seek new and better ways to serve others along your chosen path. Act as a servant to those who use your services or goods. At the same time, keep your mind eager and whetted for greater and larger opportunities, and for better ways to provide service."

I could only reply in a tone that was born of doubt, **"Could it really be that simple?"**

"Indeed, consider your own experience: When you mortgaged Lumber Mill No. 2, did you not seek more prestige than you had earned? In later employment, did you not seek greater compensation for less service?"

**"Sir, I don't understand. Because, while I wanted to show the heirs that I could exceed their efforts, I was also hungry to serve."**

The caller's response was unwavering, "No, William, this is a contradiction! You see, in these instances, you failed to act as a servant. A servant always seeks to provide more good, greater value and superior service than his or her compensation. Only the fool expects compensation or authority beyond the good he provides. And, if they receive greater payment or higher status, it will always be fleeting and short-lived. Predictably, it will take flight from their hands almost as quickly as it was found."

**"Sir, I –",** my mouth dropped. Unable to understand what the caller was telling me, I pleaded, **"I am afraid that I do not understand."**

"Remember, I told you that this is a Universe of order! Everything works with immense accuracy and according to these laws! The accuracy of these forces is so precise that even the finest crafted clock pales one thousand fold in comparison!

"When you try to obtain money or acclaim beyond the good you provide, it will always take flight from your hands. It may be swift or it may be gradual, but it is the unfailing nature of the Universe to re-distribute such things to those who justly earn them. This is why people who seek riches or any compensation without a true desire to provide service can only fail. Anything unearned shall eventually leave your grasp. It will be redistributed, **it will be all gone...all gone!"**

Just as the caller uttered these last words, a clock on a nearby tower began to chime. The clock rang out with a distinct *"Ding-Dong," "Ding-Dong,"* as we entered the midnight hour. It seemed as if the clock was secretly nodding in agreement, a dramatic reverberation of the caller's last words. The clock tower's tune and the caller's warnings rang like a chorus in my mind: *"Ding-Dong, all gone, Ding-Dong, all gone, all gone."* This hypnotic refrain was only interrupted when the caller began to speak again,

"Mark these words well: Doing less and demanding more puts you in conflict with all forces of natural law. Like a man trying to swim against the powerful currents of the sea, such effort always results in a person's failure and eventual destruction."

No sooner than the last word was spoken, a tall, thin man, with a strange appearance, approached our carriage. The man had quick-darting eyes, and a long, drawn face that reminded me of a leather pelt, dried, yellowed and then stretched to its maximum. He wore a very nice and expensive jacket, and even pants with cuffs. Yet, all of his garments were ragged, dirty and generally neglected. Certainly, my clothing was pitiable, but something else beyond his garments caught my attention. I had the sense that he was wholly distressed about something. Just then, a low, raspy sound slithered from the tall man's mouth,

"W-why y-o-u-n-g m-a-n, might you know what the t-i-m-e would be?"

The caller never took its eyes from the front of the carriage, but I blurted out:

"According to the clock tower, the time is just past 12 o'clock a.m., Sir!"

With this, the tall man quickly scampered away into the darkness. I remember thinking it strange that a matter so pressing would occupy a man at this hour. It also seemed odd that this man wore nice garments, yet, each appeared so filthly and untidy. Yet, still another question burned in my mind:

**"Sir, why didn't this man hear the chimes of the clock tower?"** I asked.

"Each person lives in a different reality, William, don't forget this fact," the caller explained.

As the man sank back into the shadows, we slowly followed him some distance behind.

Eventually, the man disappeared into a corner building off Main Street. I could hear his hurried footsteps climbing a flight of noisy, wooden steps within the building. We parked alongside a street lamp, and waited. Again, I sat in confusion and sought clarification from the caller:

**"Sir, what of this man?"**

"William, this man began life in poverty. He built a thriving business and was quite successful for a time."

**"Of course, this man must have vital business at this late hour! His urgency demonstrates his desire to serve. Perhaps, he is attending a meeting of his stockholders,"** I reasoned.

"William, this man was late for a game of gambling," the caller said, in concerned tone. "The upstairs of that building is a concealed betting and gaming house. Each dollar he once earned providing service to others, is now quickly fleeing from his hands. Unless his beliefs and actions change, his last dollar will be squandered and lost by the end of the month."

**"Sir"** I said with my mouth dropping wide open, **"how did this man reach such a point? You told me he had built a thriving business at one time!"**

"It began as most things do, as a simple seed of thought," said the caller.

**"Yes, but what seed could have turned his fortunes so?"**

"William, this man began to question why his investments did not turn a profit even more quickly."

**"But, if he had a desire to rise, then he should have risen indeed. What did he do wrong?"** I inquired.

"Alas, he did what many people do, he gave power to his lesser self, and soon it guided his steps," the caller instructed.

**"Since he was quite successful,"** I said with eyes fixed on the concealed gaming house **"he must have understood these rules. How could he have later forgotten them?"**

"The destructive self is very unassuming in its ways. His first thoughts centered on why his business was not profiting as quickly as he desired. Then, instead of looking for ways to provide better service, he sought answers from his lesser self. You see, he blamed those around him."

**"Did he blame his employees?"** I pursued.

"Yes, he did, but he also blamed the world he lived in. He blamed the taxes and tariffs he had to pay. He blamed the regulations, which required him to pay decent wages and soon cut into his worker's pay envelope. He then created schemes to avoid paying taxes. He began to question why his customers did not buy more of his services, and soon he chided them for it. Now, at this late hour, he squanders his last savings attempting to balance the scales by gambling. But you see, by acting against all fundamental truths, one will only be doomed to fail."

With an exclamation of frustration, I yelped, **"But what should this man have done to expand his business?"**

"He should have remembered this simple truth: you only increase by providing greater service to others. Everything of value is obtained by serving others. This growth may be material, it may be spiritual, or even both. It you want greater income, follow the laws. If you want greater fulfillment and understanding, follow the laws. With a focus on service, opportunities will abound and constantly multiply.

"For, an unstoppable cause for advancement is a heart dedicated to service, and a mind fixed upon the highest levels of achievement. Please hear me well, because nothing can hold such a person back, yet millions still try to get something for nothing."

**"Sir, if no one receives something for nothing"** I said staunchly, **"then what about the criminal who steals a fortune and lives to tell the tale?"**

"What of the criminal who steals his fortune and lives to tell the tale?" the caller answered calmly. "Only the foolish will believe that he is beyond this rule. Do not be misled, because while he may never be locked in a physical prison, the criminal is always an inmate of his own mind. Guilt, imaginings and paranoia always shall keep him from true happiness. Because he knows no other means to achieve his needs, he will continue to serve the destructive self. And service to the destructive self will compel further crimes or association with others who also hold these destructive thoughts.

"The criminal's service to the destructive self and his ignorance of natural law will place all forces of the Universe against him. It is unquestionable that the only result shall be the tolling of his death bell.

"At the same time, when you provide greater service to others and focus on high achievement, eventually you can have anything that you truly desire."

The caller's eyes then met mine, but, in return, I could only look downward. My mind, once more, began to dwell on fear, and I moaned. Then, with quivering lips, spoke again,

**"But, Sir, I live with only the rags on my back!"** My head now hung from my neck like a heavy steel block, and I groused, **"How can I serve others if I can barely care for myself?"**

"You will never rise above your current state until you begin to serve and give to others. What of your actions now? What service do you provide? Do you give or do you only ask?"

The caller paused, and I pondered its last words. It was then that an illumination came upon me that was so blinding and overwhelming that its radiance nearly cast me from the seat of the carriage. I carefully looked back upon my life and, in every situation it was true that as I gave less service, my rewards and happiness soon disappeared. This held true for financial rewards. Yet, it also held true for more important non-material rewards, such as peace, contentment, fulfillment and love. The law of cause and effect revealed itself once more in my life. It was a truth that was so powerful, so enduring, and I had forgotten it.

I raised my head up once more and the caller continued, "No one receives something for nothing, of course, you may receive a penny or morsel in charity, but you have not earned them. As a result, these handouts are soon bitter fruit to you. Did you not scowl at those who gave you this charity? Without giving something of yourself, each penny you receive and each morsel you consume will only increase your pain and your emptiness. Soon, unearned money or a lack of true giving causes a person to fall deeper and deeper into a self-created abyss. Do you recognize why this is true?"

**"I see now that service will allow me to advance,"** I said. Yet, with my hand over my mouth and in nearly the same breath, I whispered, "but the lack of service can't make all things bitter."

The caller heard my words and its quick response startled me. "Of course, the lack of service can make all things bitter," the caller countered.

"First, remember that you will never receive real payment when no service is rendered. No one ever receives something of value without paying a corresponding price. The greedy child who inherits a fortune may squander it quickly or find that he has little purpose, drive or satisfaction. Unearned money and wealth can never bring reason, will or fulfillment. Just as rest after a hard days work can be delightful, without work this rest becomes sloth and may only bring gloom. All unearned things can become as vitriolic as poison."

I rubbed my chin and paused as I thought about its words. And, soon before me, I saw the many faces of my past associates. Routinely, their bovine-like eyes would transform and twinkle as they spoke of unearned payments, swindled rewards and stolen items. Before me, they smiled and raised their glasses high, celebrating the latest hornswoggle and theft. It was a common belief that such things would place them ahead of the fools who worked and earned. Yet, no matter their happiness in those moments, it seemed that negative fates and, sometimes, horrible reversals eventually befell them all. I quickly traced and recounted the demise of each of them. Then, their faces disappeared and vanished, like parting fog in the night air.

**"Sir, are those who seek unearned payment, subject to an accounting?"**

"Unearned payment exacts a heavy toll," added the caller. "This price shall be paid in misery. Never forget that it is only the hand and heart of one busily engaged in providing service to others that will produce real happiness and deliver alignment with your true self."

**"Sir, is this why I felt greater pain and sadness, no matter how much charity I received?"**

"Yes, this is the reason!" exclaimed the caller. "Remember, the greatest forces of the Universe all begin from the inside and then proceed outward. If you want fulfillment but give nothing of yourself, then you are operating in a backward fashion. Assume you wanted a warming fire? Would you wait by an empty stove and demand heat? One might consider such a person insane, yet, people act in this manner daily.

"Remember, you can only receive heat by acting first! You must first provide the fuel. Only then, could the stove bring you heat. You cannot expect payment, unless you give of yourself and provide service.

"Similarly, you cannot expect true fulfillment when you give nothing of yourself. Happiness is created by giving. Kindness and giving are the fuels which creates life's fulfillment, life's excitement, and life's miracles. It can never be created by unearned compensation, just as a hot stove cannot be created without first adding logs or fuel. Throughout the ages, countless people have searched first for money, happiness or both. If they look first to serve with love, then they shall find both."

I began to understand the caller's words and they made great sense to me. Yet, deep at my core, I could not release the grip that fear held on me. It seemed that, despite the caller's reassurance, I knew that I had nearly nothing to offer. I reasoned that if value must first be given, and I was indeed penniless, it was wise to wait until my circumstances changed before trying to serve anyone. I suspected the caller would understand my reasoning, so I said:

**"Yes, but, since my body is weak and I am hungry, I cannot serve anyone. When I am able to obtain food and shelter, then, I will serve."**

The caller replied, elegantly, "So you would shiver by an empty stove, hoping that chance might somehow fill it with wood?

Don't be misled; such a day will never come! And if it does, then what happens when all the fuel is burned? What then?

"Those who understand these rules will always provide service to others first, rather than expecting others to serve them. To accomplish this, be wise, and organize your purpose and thought. Make use of any meager tools or simple means available to you. Almost immediately, you will awake one morning and find that you have been given greater means. You will turn the corner and find additional opportunity. You will look around you and uncover more bountiful resources. The person who delivers more service than expected always finds this miracle of increase in their outer world, while the person who does not only finds increasing lack."

As much as I tried, I could not imagine helping anyone in my current condition. With my hands motioning widely about my face, I interjected,

**"I cannot, Sir!"** My voice began to crackle and fear seemed to be consuming each breath, **"my body h–hungers and I feel weak."**

"Hear me well!" the caller interjected. "Remember, nature penalizes one for idleness and misuse. Your physical body does hunger, but your greatest pain, every person's greatest pain, always comes from the continued separation from their true self, the person they were created to become."

The caller would not rest until its message was clear, "All the forces of the Universe begin inward and proceed outward. Do you understand? This is why the greatest creations, acts of charity, and accomplishments can only start as a dream, an idea, and a seedling."

I nodded my head in half-hearted agreement, but was confused.

"Failure to understand this rule is the greatest agony of all people. No person, object, or feast can satisfy this hunger for you. This hunger may only be fed from within. *You know that there is something that only you can provide and create.* You feel it in your moments of great happiness and joy; you know that it is there.

"This is who you truly are! This is your unique contribution to the world around you. Follow the rules we have been speaking of and connect with me. Even if the task is routine or mundane and not your highest aspiration, do place your unique value into it. Don't ever forget that, as you do with small things, you will do with everything"

**"It does make sense, Sir"** I replied, **"but how does putting my effort into small, modest things result in more opportunity?"**

"Each person is solely responsible for promoting themselves to their highest aspiration. This is why the wise person directs his hands and heart to work efficiently at all times. The watchful eyes of the manager are of no consequence to this individual, because he knows that he is solely responsible for promoting himself. Even if his current position or job is not ideal, he will deliver value to everyone around him. This is not because *of where he is*, but because *of what he is!* What he is arises from his dominant thinking and his actions, his consciousness. *What he is* charges the field of energy around him and changes his place in the greater field, the master field. *What he is* causes him to occupy a place where others like him are found. Soon, ideal opportunities arise from a place others call 'nowhere'. This person will cast off lowly conditions like old, tattered gloves. Nothing on earth could stop this movement, except, of course, himself.

If you accept this truth, then you will be ready to understand one of the mechanisms which cause it to be so."

Dumbfounded and uncertain, I responded, **"Sir, I do not understand what you speak of. What is the mechanism?"**

"William, the wise person knows that each seed of good planted, without being asked, will return to the planter tenfold the original seed. For example, the farmer acts in faith and plants many seeds. Soon, he is blessed with an orchard of trees yielding countless fruits. Each tree grew from only one seed, yet, it produces multiple returns. The farmer acted in faith of this universal rule and is soon rewarded tenfold, twentyfold, one hundredfold and beyond. Service, which goes further than the expectations of others, will always produce multiple returns.

"Did you begin work at the docks from your own initiative, or did you wait for guaranteed payment? In your labor at the docks, you offered more service than you were asked, correct? You also offered assistance to each person around you, did you not? As a result, you quickly advanced. Your heart was dedicated to service and, soon, you caught the attention of those whose thoughts aligned with yours. For example, Mr. Wells recognized your great power, did he not? This is called the law of 'multiple returns' and, at one time, you used it to benefit yourself and those all around you.

"Yet, this law of multiple returns has its opposite, because, at the same time, the foolish person always tries to attain more payment, prestige or authority than they have earned. As a consequence, they propel themselves downward, with increasing swiftness, at all times."

Nodding my head in agreement, I said, **"Yes, it was first the owner of the vessel who noticed my service. Then, it was Mr. Wells, who called me to his office in December of that year."**

The caller placed a firm hand on my shoulder, and said, "All truly successful people have mastered the law of multiple returns. Logically, these people can quickly identify anyone with the same heart of a servant, and a like mind directed toward the highest levels of achievement. A person will always advance, not because of *where they are*, luck or circumstance, but, because of *what they are!*"

I began to shake my head left to right, **"What a mysterious force this –"**

The caller broke in, "William, there is no mystery!"

**"Sir, is this the reason why, in these years, I have only encountered people with the same hopeless, desperate, and defeated temperament as I? It appeared to me that this was the natural order of things."**

"It is never the natural order to think and then live in such chaos. You concentrated upon hopeless thinking and this brought you others who think in this manner."

**"Did I send a message to all those around me?"**

"Of course, you did! You thought of defeat and gloom, and this brought you others with the same illogical thinking. Yet, at another time in your life, you chose to think of prosperity and advancement. You chose to act with the heart of a servant. When this was done, you became a powerful beacon of light. You moved yourself to a plane and level of awareness held by those who shared this thinking: the owner of the vessel, the berth manager, Mr. Wells and others.  People and opportunities which provided advancement came forward, at every turn."

With these words, the caller was silent.  As my mind absorbed these latest revelations, I looked past our carriage car.  I noticed that the low-lying night fog had now paired with the light of the street lamp.  This combination caused the area around us to shine in a golden tint.  Just then, from the doorway of the building, the tall man walked out into the street.  The modest yellow color that once filled his face had now departed and his cheeks seemed to drip like muddy sludge from his eye sockets.  His expression now appeared almost like a mourning skeleton.  Even his narrow shoulders drooped down further than before.  He looked funereal and heartbroken.  Immediately, I thought of the caller's warnings.

I lunged to the rear of the carriage to tell him of my new discoveries.  Before I could say a word to him, he disappeared into the shadows, outside the golden radiance of the lamp.  I called out to him many times, and even searched for him in the darkness, but, he could not be found at this time.

# CHAPTER TWENTY-FIVE

# What is Your Inventory?

THE STOREKEEPER STRAIGHTENED HIS SMALL, RED bow tie as if a thorough inspection of his trim and dress were about to occur. "This new year will be the busiest and most productive yet!" he exclaimed. He then imagined a vast crowd of customers moving in and out of his store. He saw these customers personally thanking him for his fair prices and extra service. He felt the pride of knowing that he always gave his customers a little something extra in their bag. It may be a small bit of candy for their child, or a new sample spice, tea or other offering.

Row-by-row and isle-by-isle, he counted each item in his store. On a small, lined, paper tablet, he put a number beside each article, to indicate his supply. He took great satisfaction in knowing exactly what he had in stock. If he needed a new product or dry good to satisfy his patrons, then he quickly found ways to obtain it. "The more I know what I have, the better I can serve them," he said to himself. "If I don't have a particular item, I can always find a way to obtain it!" When those last words were spoken, he performed a short dance and giggled with joy.

I SOON FOUND THAT WE WERE BACK ON MAIN Street, re-tracing the path we had taken earlier that night. As the carriage made its way along the cobblestone street, I decided that I must make these lessons part of my life. With determination and resolve, I asked the caller:

**"Sir, I must apply these lessons. What shall I do first?"**

"Just as you receive these words, start to use the power of thankfulness and gratitude," replied the caller.

**"What is this power? How do I use it?"**

"Ask yourself, could a merchant offer her goods to the public if she does not have an inventory of her stock? To use the power of thankfulness and gratitude, you must, right now, at this moment, take inventory and appreciate the great gifts you already possess."

Just then, we passed the window of the dry goods store, where earlier in the night the disheveled man stood. With the carriage now parked, the caller and I watched the neat storekeeper with the small red bow tie. The storekeeper's head was held even higher than before. He seemed incredibly happy and, by accounts, he was in his own blissful paradise. Up and down, left and right, he pranced around his store. All the while, he took inventory of his wares and he smiled more and more.

"How strange it is," I said, rubbing my eyes, "it looks like he is planning and preparing as if a great flood of people will arrive at any moment."

The golden light from his window surrounded our carriage, with a warm radiance. I felt inspired and secure for a moment, as you can imagine. However, my ego began to compare myself to the storekeeper. With my eyes off the window, I looked down at my torn and threadbare pants, and remembered how little in material possessions I owned. It was then that a familiar haunting came over me, once more. In contrast to the neat storekeeper, I seemed quite poor and had nearly nothing to offer. My head sunk down lower and I closed my eyes.

"Listen!" the caller said, interrupting my gloom, "change your beliefs and cast your sights upward! Appreciate and be thankful for the power and the good that you possess *right now*. Indeed, you may have few material possessions tonight, but you have infinite power within you…you are an infinite power!"

I raised my head slowly and began to listen as the caller continued,

"Understand that a person who continually thinks of how little they have will always seek outward objects, people, and situations to make them happy and content. If you think in this manner, then you have no understanding of your true inner power. As a result, you will always divert, neglect and misuse it!"

Of course, you might try to argue that it was experience, money, opportunity, or time that you lacked. All of these are lies."

**"But, Sir, how would gratitude make me different?"**

"With gratitude, you go about your day focusing and using the good that you already possess. And, like clockwork, you are always given more. This is perfect harmony with the workings of the Universe, because true power and lasting joy always start from within and then proceed outward! Remember, it is *not where you are, but what you are!*"

A clouded state came over me and, again, I was confused. Just as you might, I sought more clarification, **"You say I should** be grateful, but what assets do I have? I have no money, no inventory, and no one to serve at this moment?"

"At this time, you may have little money, but your inventory is strength of body and the faculties of your wonderful mind. Some men and women have changed history, built vast fortunes and benefited countless in pain, starting with even less than what you now enjoy!

"Never forget that you have ownership of your body and your mind. These are some of the most magnificent possessions you will ever be given. Your mind will act as your obedient and untiring servant. It can connect you to all power, all knowledge and all wisdom. It can and it will bring anything you truly desire.

"With this mind, you have the same power which has created the great industrialists, heads of state, activists, humanitarians and inventors. You hold a power that can topple all barriers, advance all people, and change the world. All of this is at your disposal."

The caller then inched its face close to mine, and whispered, "But, listen closely and never forget these words: *This power can only come forward when you call it to action.*"

**"But, Sir!"** I replied, slowly shaking my head. **"If I am thankful, won't I then become too content? Won't the person with thankfulness lose this desire?"**

"While gratitude and thanks are recognition of the good you already have, they can never cause one to lay idle. If you have true gratitude, then you will take inventory and appreciate the gifts you already possess. By the same token, you will understand the amazing worth and value of these gifts. You will know that these gifts should never be wasted, and that each should be used to serve others."

**"B-but how do I develop my gifts?"**

"Development and growth only come when your gifts are shared with others, practiced and expanded upon. A mind focused on service provides the best path to development. A desire to serve others beyond yourself will always cause you to grow and advance, even if your individual needs are completely met."

As these words were spoken, the carriage began moving again, and we left the neat storekeeper. The caller continued,

"This man has the most profitable store in the entire district, but he is also the most successful."

**"Sir, you have made it sound like success and profit are different things? If he is the most profitable, isn't he automatically the most successful?"** I pondered.

"Hardly!" the caller now let out a bellowing laugh. "This man is successful because he loves the service he provides through his business. He is profitable for the same reason, but profit does not equal success."

As the carriage traveled eastward, I thought of the storekeeper and the pleasure he gave to his work. I imagined how wonderful it might feel if I could do the same. Yet, still another question still burned in my mind:

**"Sir, I hope you don't tire of my questioning, but, in these years my mind drifts to thoughts of sadness, lack, and my painful memories. At most times, I feel that I am unable to control it, to direct it."**

The caller replied, "A mind with no desire, objective or plan will always fall victim to ideas of sadness, lack and pain. The reason is that nature requires humans to utilize their minds. The penalty for non-use is weakness, deterioration and negativity. As a result, anything which is not utilized and not progressing shall slowly crumble."

The caller then pointed its cane towards the east, "Imagine the farmer who tills the soil in the field, but plants no crops. What do you suppose he will find?"

**"Sir, I suspect weeds, rubbish and undesirables would soon be found."**

"Of course, such a farmer would always find weeds in his field!" the caller replied.

The caller then tapped its cane on the floorboard of the carriage to make sure my attention was keenly focused, and said, "The same is true for the idle mind. There are no exceptions. The mind is always fertile and will expand and multiply anything you feed it."

**"Sir, I understand!  Indeed, then my next task shall be to obtain a desire for something in life?"** I asked.

"Indeed, you are correct! Your victory will come when you direct all of your energy and actions toward the attainment of an ideal, purpose or desire.  It may be a simple goal or a lofty one, but it must be something you greatly desire.  Once you can apply this process to simple things, you will lay the foundation for greater triumphs and successes.  In this, your future pattern for growth and fulfillment has been forged."

The caller paused for a moment and I felt a knot of anxiousness in my stomach, and I knew another vital message was nearing.   Then, with its face close to mine, the caller slowly mouthed each of the following words with careful precision:

"Blaze these words in your mind, for if you use this knowledge you can create anything you desire: Concentrate vividly upon having obtained your objective. Smell the fragrances, feel the feelings and hear the sounds associated with your desired outcome. Do this over and over again, and live at this moment. It shall soon be that the image and feelings of victory shall be so real, that your current reality is blended with what you seek. When this blending occurs, you have now become one with what you are seeking. Then, follow your instincts and act to serve others. Do not be content to merely dream about your future desires, act on them! Dreaming or thinking without action can never result in creation."

The caller then said, "If you forget all you have learned on this night, please never surrender what I am now about to tell you."

I responded, quickly, **"Sir, I shall remember with all my might. I shall!"**

"Listen closely, for the greatest people of all time have learned one common truth: The mind must always maintain a picture of the result, circumstance or opportunity it seeks. This mental image of the desired outcome must be maintained. The image and feelings in your mind must be so strong that you see and feel this future reality taking place now. *This type of action will change precisely what you are and how you view the world.* It is then, that you *will soon* occupy a place in your outer reality that matches exactly what you hold in your inner reality."

**"Sir, is this why the storekeeper was happily preparing for a great flood of customers, yet, no customers were in sight?"**

The caller was silent for a time and the carriage continued along Main Street. Just when I began to suspect that I was in error, the caller turned its face to me. A wide smile cascaded across its thin mouth, as it said, "You are beginning to see the forces at work around you, excellent!"

## CHAPTER TWENTY-SIX
# *What is Your Watermark?*

"**S**IR, SIR, I FEEL MY HEART POUNDING WITH excitement. Please tell me what must I do after I have solidified these desires and feelings in my mind?"

"Don't ever forget that thoughts and feelings must always be met with action. You must place unrelenting action behind your thoughts and feelings. Act to make your desires and feelings an absolute reality. Always act in faith and, if guided by your higher self, move forward without delay. If you feel discouraged or downtrodden, use your mental imagery to feel and create the future realization of this desire in your mind, today. Don't ever sit inactive! Those who sit idle or only wish for better circumstances will decompose and perish like rotting fruit! Hold what you desire in your mind and then serve others as you work to create it around you!"

"**While I may take action and create the desires in my heart, what shall I do if failure greets me?**"

"Realize that temporary defeat and failure will undoubtedly greet you at different times. Consider this: How will you know which actions are improper unless failure has sent you its message? This is the only way for you to know which actions are proper and which are not. Failure will soon become a benefit, if you allow it to temper and shape your resolve and to prove the worth of your actions. When you meet with failure, question the reason; question its cause. Then, simply change actions again until they are proper."

**"Sir, you speak as if failure is temporary. Is this true?"**

"Of course, it is temporary! To all those who understand how the Universe operates, failure can be nothing but temporary. Once you continue forward, failure is a fleeting moment now long past. Like the morning fog, it departs almost as quickly as it arrived. Yet, for those who quit and accept defeat, failure becomes a suffocating cloud which looms at all hours, in all places. Soon, it penetrates all areas of their life. Remember, if you yield to failure, you will soon find that it spreads quickly and has become your master."

**"But, why should I fail, if I am serving my true self? It would seem that I would meet with success, time and time again."**

"Impossible and illogical!" the caller said, loudly. "Failure is not denial; it is only preparation for greater victory. The person destined for greatness cannot claim greatness without paying nature's price.

"One may think they serve their true self, but most people are not able to clearly hear its message. Early in your journey, you will be unable to discern between proper and improper action.

"Failure allows you to clarify these voices and to extract only the true messages of your higher self. This is why one should never run from failure without seeking its lesson. If you run, you will only meet with the same circumstance time and time again, in a never-ending spiral of agony, torment and defeat."

The caller stopped the carriage, and turned its torso to directly face me. Again, it placed its powerful hand on my neck and shoulder, and said:

"William, your connection to me will only become stronger by understanding the meaning of failure. Failure is an opportunity to reinforce our communication, and to channel more of my power in preparation for the great moments that await you.

"When you meet failure, consider the source of the obstacle. Permanent barriers to what you desire are never found in the outside world, but are only alive in your mind. These obstacles are nourished by limited thinking and erroneous beliefs.

"You must find the source of the limiting belief. If a person was involved in the creation of this belief *forgive and release them. Then forgive yourself.* Seek out new beliefs and then hold to your purpose with an even greater hunger. Do not dwell on such failure, but devour its lesson."

I began to feel that I could try again, but, as much as I wanted to look upon failure as a source of inspiration and direction, it seemed difficult. The pain of my past was still sharp and stinging, and a part of me delighted in serving it up again and again like an unending plate of food. As I consumed it, my once-flowing energy slowed like molasses. I shook my head, and said:

**"Oh, Sir, at one time I believed myself knowledgeable. But, now, I find little knowledge and only memories of mistakes."**

"Do not listen to your lesser self!" the caller demanded. "Change the meaning of failure and, immediately, your energy will rise!  Remember, in order to reach the desires of your heart, you will also need wisdom.  Wisdom does not come from success.  Wisdom is born of defeat, and claimed by an iron will and persistence.  Any person can acquire knowledge through action and study.  Yet, to stand with the greats, you must have wisdom.

"To obtain wisdom, you must face failure, extract its lesson and build an unrelenting resolve to press forward.  Almost immediately, this resolve will be shown in your person, and glow: the certainty with which you speak, the quickness of your step, and the confidence in your decisions.  Everything about you will exude this wisdom and power.

"As you go through life, others will recognize these traits in you.  Soon, greater successes and opportunities will come forward, and then, lo, the impossible shall be done!"

**"But, Sir,"** I responded in frustration, **"negative thoughts creep into my mind at strange hours, places, and moments.  I have tried desperately to control them, yet, my first thoughts are always negative and saddening."**

"William, a mind with no purpose or passion will always be drawn toward negative thoughts and circumstances.  Yet, if you have identified a purpose or desire and negative thoughts still come, then you must examine *your rules*, your subconscious beliefs."

**"What if a person does not know their beliefs, Sir?"**

"Then, this person will lose control of their life.  Beliefs are the factories of thought, and their products should concern you very much.  Negative beliefs must be removed from your mind, because every destructive or negative belief you hold can only return to you a negative thought.

"For example, do you believe that you can create the desires held in your mind?  Do you believe that people are inherently good, or are all people evil? Do you believe that sufficient opportunity exists for everyone, or do you believe that happiness and prosperity are only reserved for a select few?

"All of these deep-seated beliefs are numerous rules you have created between yourself and the outside world. *You create your life experience according to what you believe about yourself and the world around you.*

"These beliefs soon entrench themselves and produce similar thoughts and control your actions. Right now, begin to examine your day-to-day thoughts about your life, other people, and the future. This will allow you to identify your deep-seated beliefs."

**"What shall I do next, Sir?"**

"When any destructive thought comes, pull it from the garden of your mind. Like a farmer who encounters weeds in his field, you must follow each thought down to its roots and then trace these roots to their origin. Its origin shall be a destructive belief. You must identify these negative or limiting beliefs, and then change them. Like tearing the wings from a beautifully-feathered eagle, limiting beliefs will force even the noblest creature to drop and wallow on the filthiest and slimy grounds."

**"Should I do this regularly, Sir?"**

"Whenever a negative thought comes, ask your mind to uncover the deep belief behind this thought. Ask your mind what steps are needed to release you from this deep belief. The answers will come so follow them! Then immediately replace the negative thought with the opposite empowering thought and then forgive the past situations that gave rise to your deep belief. Then forgive yourself.

"Imagine, if you fed your physical body poison, wouldn't you remove it quickly? The mind and the diet of thought it consumes are no different. Most would never consume poison, but they are unable to identify the slow poisoning of their minds. Continue to do this until your mind is aligned with proper thinking. In this manner, the foundation for a grand and unlimited life is created."

The carriage began moving again and we sat quieted for a brief time. From a distance, I began to see familiar alleyways and lampposts. I knew the Custom House would be close by. As we drew closer, the caller leaned over and spoke to me,

"With the passing of one more block, we shall be in the location where we started. Perhaps, you will learn a few things at this corner."

The carriage then came to a standstill. As I knew this area of the city very well, I doubted that there could be any lessons to glean from this particular corner. Nevertheless, I looked around and soon noticed something strikingly unfamiliar!

On the south side of the street, I saw a man sitting in a merchant store. He wore a tidy white shirt and neat, brown, short pants. He was positioned at a small writing table and reading from a stack of books. A single, crooked candle slowly sputtered waves of light across his modest study area. He was reading intently and seemed to be enjoying himself very much.

Just as soon as I had seen him, the man leaned back in a long careful stretch and grinned widely to himself. It appeared that he was thinking of something that gave him great pleasure. He then bent forward and carefully placed an opulent, but frayed, burgundy ribbon between the browned pages of a book. He closed its faded leather cover and blew out the candle.

Quickly, I sought clarification, **"Is that man the shop owner?"**

"No, William, he is a factory worker and he was, at one time, a young orphan just as you were."

**"Yes, but what is he doing in that store?"** I probed.

"I am glad you noticed him. He offered value to the storekeeper, and now he is allowed to sleep in the store at night. He watches over it, and cleans the aisles and shelves. After he is finished, he is also allowed to read from the storekeeper's personal library."

**"Sir, if he works in a factory during the day, then why can't he afford lodging?"**

"Indeed, he can afford other lodging, but, at the present time, he is saving money, providing a service, and has access to a small collection of books. All of this opposed to merely paying for lodging."

**"What does he do with this money he saves?"** I asked.

"He is able to use his money to purchase more books and some additional schooling. You see, he will not be a factory worker much longer."

**"Sir, please tell me more."**

"It is true that this man currently has little material possessions. He labors long hours and dislikes his work. Yet, this man does not dwell on the hopelessness, disparity and lack around him. To the contrary, the deplorable conditions of the harsh factory stir in him an incredible hunger for aesthetics, wisdom, strength and equity. He repeatedly conditions his mind to search for these ideals within his world and, lo, they do appear! You see, William, he presented a question to his mind: 'How can I make use of the talents I already have, while developing new ones?'

"And like a faithful servant, his mind presented to him a flood of answers. As you have seen, he is following the instructions of his true self. Surely, his work at the factory consumes his time, but he makes use of what little extra time is his own. You can see that he was reading at this late hour. In the quiet solitude of the merchant store, his mind sees and feels great accomplishments. To him, these images and events are as real as the seat you and I are sitting on. And, indeed, they are very real. Mark these words well: *While he does not wish for his present position, he does not define himself by it!*"

The caller then looked sternly at me, and said, "This man is connected to his true self, his creative self, and it will provide him with everything he seeks."

**"Sir, what was he reading at this late hour?"**

"At the present time, he feverishly reads stories of great men and women who yielded power in a fair manner, and to the betterment of humankind. He reads of the great philosophers, statesmen, and humanitarians. And, William, soon he will begin to associate with others in this community who share these same ideals.

"He sets his mind fiercely to these elevated ideas, and he gives no shred of thought to compromise. In fact, this man is not just reading about the greats, but he envisions himself acting with them, standing among them. He feels the moments of these great triumphs, today. He basks in the warmth and revels in the glory of a future that cannot be denied him. He allows this script to unfold in his mind, over and over again. It penetrates every cell of his body and charges the field around him. As he does this, an unstoppable unity is established. In all of this, he is eliciting his creative being to work tirelessly and transform his ideals into reality."

**"Does he ever leave the factory?"**

"In a sense, he has already left the harsh factory. His mind is no longer chained by limiting beliefs or directed by the foreman's bell. His mind has taken its wings and moved him beyond it. His body will follow very soon!

"One day, you will see him again. He will be a leader and will advance freedom, fair working conditions and opportunity for all men and women. His true self would not and could not fail him. His higher self acted as his loyal servant and, with an unerring love and direction, it clothed him, nourished him and allowed him the realization of all the grandest desires of his heart."

The caller paused for a moment and then pointed to the now dark merchant store, with its cane, "Mark these words well: **The tides of advancement must rise to the great watermark which he set in his mind!**"

With one of its fingers pointed toward my forehead, the caller then added, "Never neglect this truth: **The only limits are those established in the mind** and while each person sets their own limits, the most amazing truth is that no limit ever exists."

Ask yourself: *What limits have you set for yourself and for your life? Certainly, I did not give them to you. Do you know of their source?*

A CHILL OF EXCITEMENT OVERTOOK MY BODY AND I began to imagine myself one day as this man was. I envisioned myself in great places and serving others in great ways. With my mind elevated to this blissful state, I continued to ask questions of the caller:

**"Sir, what of the person who serves both selves for a time? What may become of this person?"**

"A person who serves the creative and destructive self will stagnate for a time, but eventually they can only decline. Always remember this: **The tides of advancement will only rise to the watermark you set in your mind."**

With great emotion the caller continued, "Consider another man who toils in a harsh and unfair factory, who has little prospects of a material nature. This man labors long hours and loathes his work, yet, he faithfully remains at this work, for he is good of heart. This man does not fashion any dream or ideal for his life, and time passes quickly. Soon, he gives up on wanting more and simply decides to endure his vocation. Yet, as most do, he becomes determined to enjoy his precious leisure time.

"If he controls his thoughts, then he can maintain the employment he dislikes for the remainder of his years, but he is limited. Understand this well: If one loathes their work, then they cannot continually increase their service to others. This will keep such a person in a trade or position they despise for the remainder of their years, or until their thoughts change.

"Even worse, this man's contempt for his work will cause self-doubt, frustration and unhappiness. This dislike will saturate his mind, even during leisure hours. Soon, leisure time will only bring him a feeling of hopelessness and dread, as he waits for the inevitable workday and dreary life which follow. This man's ignorance of natural law will cause him to believe that real happiness and true joy are impossible. He may believe that true peace, fulfillment and wisdom are relics of years past. People who fall into this trap may die toiling in an occupation that they despise, and living with inner turmoil and self-doubt. Most will never rise to the highest levels of happiness and deep contentment.

"Was it education, skill, or family background that held this man back? No, it was his failure to create a central direction and desire in his life. His fate was certain because he did not command a greater vision and a greater share for himself.

"During all of those cold loathsome mornings when he grumbled about his life, the arduous days when he labored in sadness and the nights he spent in his dark suffocating quarters as he pitied himself and wept, the higher self waited anxiously. It waited for him to call it to action. It could have provided him with all he truly desired, but this man never had enough faith in himself or anything else to connect with his true self.

"Did the world commit an injustice? No, the injustice was all his own, because *he simply failed to ask!*

"Mark these words well: **The tides of advancement can only rise to the watermark you set in your mind.**"

The caller then began to describe another situation that I knew quite well, "Assume, yet, a third man, who has little prospects of a material nature. He labors long hours and loathes his work. Sadly, this man serves his destructive self for a length of time. He begins to complain about his work and, amazingly, others who also share disdain for their employer effortlessly appear all around him.

"He begins to work less, but demand more. He believes this is appropriate for him, so he plants this thought seed in his mind. His mind nourishes this thought seed and it grows. Naturally, this man soon believes that he will gain pleasure by taking more from his employer than he is entitled to.

"This man's service to his destructive self distorts his senses so much that he sees only hopelessness, disparity, and lack all around him. Thoughts of all unfairness continue to occupy his mind until there is a singular belief that any effort is futile. This man's choice was to plant and sustain such seeds, and he now reaps the harvest! The small seed he planted and cared for now produces a bounty.

"He sinks into the depths of wretchedness. His destructive self continually seeks dominance, and it further clouds his mind. He may begin to believe that acts of theft, violence, or dishonesty are his only means of survival; the only way he can balance the scales of fortune. By careless service to his lesser self, this man has progressively lowered his expectations and desires until they are feral and equal that of an animal.

"Now, mark these words well: **The tides of advancement will certainly fall to the low watermark you set in your mind!**

"The destructive self will continue to lower this man's ideals until the result is premature death or imprisonment. In doing so, the destructive entity has completed its purpose, its highest ideal. Who called it to action? Did society inflict this injustice upon him? Was it the will of others? No, the injustice was all his own.

"Yet, people assume that life is unfair, that the world favors the rich, the young, the tall, the short, the round, the square, the man at the edge of town, or the wealthy woman. They are wrong! The world *will only and can only* favor the person who connects to their true self!"

The caller paused for a moment and then said, "The ancient peoples of this world knew well of this power. They taught that it is more influential than any earthly force. When properly understood, honored, and applied, nothing of this world could stop it. Today most have given this power over to others or buried it deep within them. It is no wonder so many are riddled with lingering fears, dis-ease, and a lack of true joy."

# CHAPTER TWENTY-SEVEN

# Giants Shall Become Ants...

WITHIN MOMENTS, THE CALLER AND I WERE standing in the same alley where our journey had begun. While I could see glimpses of the horse and carriage around the corner, the dark alley remained unchanged and purely dreadful. Again, I felt the chill of the night air. The rotting garbage choked my breathing. The damp newssheets I had once used to cover my body sat undisturbed and waiting. Even the shameful alleyway appeared to call out and ask what foolishness I had been partaking in.

As I stood in this place, a flood of dark memories washed over me. Tears of sadness welled in my eyes, and I begged the caller to understand.

**"But sir, you have an air and strength about you which has long left my body and mind, and I still cannot fathom that you would serve someone like me."**

At this suggestion, the caller took great objection and struck the ground with its cane. The blow was so immense that the earth below shook with a thunderous boom. The caller then exclaimed with such power that its sound echoed throughout the alley. I was certain that its deafening roar could be heard for ten city blocks, or more. I closed my eyes, covered my face and shivered in fear. At that moment, a most inconceivable truth, passed down from all ages of antiquity penetrated deep within me.

"Hear Me Well!" the caller roared. **"From this moment forward, cease to engage in such groveling and foolish chatter!** Do not address me with timidity. I am here to serve you!

"I am the higher self that lies within you, and lies within each person. I can make reality anything that your mind can conceive. **I am all knowledge, all power, and all strength! I do not know of weakness, limitation and lack!** I am waiting for you to take hold of my power and to use it for whatever beneficial ends you so desire!

"I am the same creative force that shaped this Universe, molded the mountains, forged canyons and set all life into motion! I am the mountains, I am the canyons, I am God Force! **If you align yourself with me, the impossible shall be accomplished and all barriers will be crushed. A path will be made where none did exist! Abundance shall arise where there was once poverty! Courage will prevail while others cower in fear! Strength will come forward when others are frail like glass! Direction will be found amidst chaos!**

"Go about your life and hold the ideals you so desire in your mind! Do not relinquish control of them, until such ideals are reality. Happiness is your birthright, yet, it is only you who may claim it!

"Do not give your attention to thoughts of fear, lack, worry, greed, laziness or failure. **Enthrone in your mind the**

**deepest desires of your heart!** Hold fast to ideals and beliefs that strengthen our connection, because I will not let you down. I will not fail you!"

The caller paused for a brief moment and then continued to address me with commanding power and certainty. I closed my eyes, not in fear this time, but only to concentrate on its great message:

**"Even in your darkest hour, you are never alone. I am always with you!** I will never abandon you, although, at times, you have abandoned me.

"Take heed of this point and commit it to memory: **The world belongs to me; therefore, it belongs to one who allows me to serve them!** I am alongside every man and woman who has attained success, harmony and fulfillment in life.

**"Build me, feed me and let me be your devoted companion for all of your days.** I will show you that the impossible may be done, all blockades will be swept away, and any giants in your path will be cast aside as ants.

"People will stare in awe of your ability and gaze in amazement at the magical life you have created. You will know that, with your invisible ally at your side, you could never fail. This is **your greatest truth!"**

As these final words were spoken, I felt a compelling power arise within my body. I, then, opened my eyes to a most astounding sight, for just a few inches in front of me, I saw the powerful and well-muscled hand of my creative being outstretched towards me. Its body was erect and it looked at me with an incredible strength in its eyes. However, within equal distance from me, I saw the hand of another form. This hand was shrunken, discolored and bone-thin, and also within my immediate grasp. It arose from the shadows and led off only into darkness. This entity uttered no words to me and offered me no wisdom.

I gazed for a moment, almost dumbfounded and frozen, as I viewed this spectacle before me. I noted that each hand was just as accessible and near as the other. To grasp one hand or the other required no greater distance, effort or aptitude. **I can say that, at this moment, the greatest truth of all humankind had now become incredibly clear.**

A desire was born in my heart. I determined, no matter the price to honor this truth. I reached out for the hand of my creative being, clenched it tightly and then closed my eyes.

I stood there for a moment, with its hand still clasped securely in mine and I re-opened my eyes. The face before me was rosy, and its cheeks were full and strong. Its eyes were hopeful, piercing and bright. Its body was stout and its shoulders were squared. It was the same age as I, but seemed years younger. The striking person before me then smiled, warmly. I felt authority, certainty and love radiating from its every fiber and every cell.

It then leaned forward and whispered the final lesson into my ear. It told of an ultimate gift that must be given in order to obtain true love and joy. The suggestion seemed so formidable and strange that I questioned it. Yet soon I had no more doubts, and I accepted the task and completed it without fail.

At that moment my body and mind transformed and the virtues which humankind has sought for centuries became unquestionably mine. When I turned my eyes once more to the caller a wonderful thing occurred! Amazingly, the shining face of the caller was now *fully and completely my own!* Within an instant, my creative self was no longer outside of my body.

# CHAPTER TWENTY-EIGHT
# Good Day to You Sir!

I AROSE THE NEXT MORNING AND FOUND MYSELF in what seemed to be another world. The same place it was, yet all of my surroundings did, indeed, appear different. I felt neither frosty nor frigid air, but warmth that penetrated my body. As I looked beyond the alley, I saw the sun shining down upon the city in a magnificent splendor. I stepped out of the alleyway, and the invigorating golden beams penetrated my skin. I felt a deep peace and an unstoppable power within me.

I had an instinct to proceed through the city, without delay. As I stepped through the busy boulevards and thoroughfares, I noticed that, indeed, there was a striking change in my frame of mind, my sentiment and even my expression. I embraced the world with a commanding grin, love, and a feeling that all the powers of the Universe were propelling me to greatness. I felt myself overflowing with unlimited authority, harmony and love. I began to think kind thoughts of each stranger who passed. I even startled myself when I began to greet passersby. In the past, such individuals certainly might have looked down upon me or failed to acknowledge my greeting. Today was different, for I was one with creative force. I was creative force! Alas, they did greet me in return, with smiles and the words, "Good day to you, Sir!" I thought of a wood-filled stove, smiled widely, and knew that I could never be permanently denied again.

❧ ❧

I PROCEEDED TO WALK BRISKLY. WITH LITTLE SLEEP and strong pangs of hunger, another man might have sought rest and sustenance. Yet, I only sought to serve the world and embrace my future. In my path, I noticed a dark and looming soul, whom I did know quite well. This man was, indeed, Karvash, whom I continued to owe a sufficient gaming debt, which was long overdue.

I cannot recall the exact events that transpired next, yet, I recall that Karvash looked my way. I remember a feeling of unlimited power and peace in that moment, and my mind dwelled upon an image of my hands grasping a rough burlap sack at the ports. In days past, this man would have seized my body and dragged me into an alley, nook or entryway, and put a sharp blade to my throat. Yet, I continued, unmoved, and with my intentions even more determined; he looked away and I walked beyond him.

I moved forward toward the port district, with a hurry in my step. I did not have a plan, yet, I continued, without time for contemplation or worry. I cannot remember the exact events which, then, did occur, but my next recollection is that of my eager hands passing a rough burlap sack to a man in a vessel below.

# Chapter Twenty-Nine
# A Message to You!

MANY YEARS HAVE PASSED SINCE THE EVENTS of that astounding night. I did rebuild my life. Through my re-birth, I sought to improve the lives and living conditions of others, as well. The words spoken in the office of Mr. Wells were not forgotten by my creative entity. I became one of the largest land developers and builders of housing in the northwest. I sought to end the poor housing conditions in all major cities, and did greatly improve the lives of thousands of men, women and children. I did, indeed, build 'decent and honest housing.'

A most interesting occurrence did occur on a cold evening in February of 1886. As this may be of interest to the reader, I shall describe it. As soon as possible, I sought to settle the gambling debts owed to Karvash. I approached him one early evening, with full payment of the debt and interest owing. I was certain it was Karvash, as his dark matted hair, scarred cheek and cold, shark-like eyes could not be mistaken. I approached him, abruptly, and said, "Karvash, I am here to repay my gaming debts, with interest!" Yet, this man did not want my money! He met my eyes in fear, and then looked away.

Could this be the same man who held a blade to my throat, on countless occasions?

I forced the currency into the front pocket of Karvash's worn coat and quickly departed. As I walked away, I thought about the field of energy described by the caller. The caller said that only a person's consciousness can change the field of energy which they occupy. When this energy field changes, it unquestionably repositions their place among the greater field. Only when this occurs, can one cast off their lowly conditions. It was clear to me, now, that nothing on earth could stop this movement, nothing except our own choices. My eyes never cast sight upon Karvash, again.

I passed the location of the old mercantile building and that forgotten alley, on various occasions, until the year 1910. In the fall of 1933, at 75 years young, I traveled to the location with Congressman Phillip Dangle, and my grandchildren. We found that the mercantile building was no longer. The grimy alleyway was no longer present, and had been built upon. The place where death and life had both courted me would never be found on any maps or photos again.

Yet, the place where life and death so courted me does still exist. This place exists on this very day, and shall continue to exist for all future generations. The place where life and death both extend their invitation may also be found by each of you, if you care to look. This battleground can be discovered by you, on this very day and at this very moment.

If you have carefully traveled along this journey, then you may wonder of the final lesson whispered into my ear. For it was this final lesson that changed all.

It was during the last moments of that amazing night, that the creative self revealed whisper by whisper the most beautifully powerful lesson of all:

"William, there is only one task that can fully release you from the age-old prison of resentment and anger. You must forgive those you believe to have wronged you. Forgive each person no matter how difficult it may seem to be. Yet most of all William, forgive...absolutely forgive yourself."

I whispered back shaking my head in bewilderment, **"Yet how may I forgive those who have hurt me?"**

"Realize that they were just as fearful as you. They were operating from their own patterns of fear just as you once did. The people who hurt you were in pain and fright themselves and you were merely in their path.

"Yet, until you forgive others and yourself, you will distort and drain your true power. Until you forgive, your true nature can never flow forth. Any stagnant foul pools of anger, resent, and guilt will be held as trapped emotion. This trapped emotion pervades the body and will ultimately destroy you. The resentment you cling to, even if slight, will absolutely block your natural state of health and well-being."

**"How may this be so?"**

"Your mind and body enter this earthly plane as untainted good and filled with radiant health. Collected anger, fears, resentment and guilt not only drain your vital power but limit your connection to love and to the light. A collection of unhealed negative emotions permeate your cells and program your subconscious toward the destruction of health and well being. This unending program can only create dis-ease in the physical body."

**"B-but"**, I stumbled aghast with confusion, **"if I forgive, does this mean others were correct in their actions?"**

"You are not condoning or approving what transpired. Forgiveness is not a pardon for them, but a gift that you bestow upon yourself. Forgiveness, if granted, is your only true release from the chains of the past. Forgiveness is the foundation for a glorious life. Collected resent is fetid garbage and muck carried into the pure glowing white fabric of the new day. Consider all those for whom you hold anger, resentment, loathing, blame and grudge and then release them all. Then, most importantly forgive...absolutely forgive yourself."

**"I shall..."**

And so in those final moments I gave myself the ultimate gift and I would never be the same.

If you have a burning desire for a positive purpose, your higher self will come forward. Follow its impulses and release yourself from the past. Regardless of whether you are age nine or ninety nine, this faithful friend will guide your mind and hands through the day-by-day steps you must take. If you don't understand its instruction, then do not be troubled. Continue to foster it, encourage it and follow its wisdom. Your creative self is waiting as a patient guide, wanting nothing more than for you to take hold and use its power.

I have lived the lessons of this narrative, yet it is time for you to take hold of what is fittingly yours. Right now there is a feeling inside of you that is building. That feeling is the urging of your higher self, the self that guided this volume into your hands. This self has been patiently waiting, with a pressing message you must hear:

*Do not believe that your best days have passed. Do not believe that happiness is a lost relic of years gone by. I was at your side in your brightest memories and at your finest hour. I have, faithfully, remained at your side, yearning above all things that you seize my power and never release it! I am your birthright, yet you are the only one who may bring me forward.*

*You are, by your very nature, a creative being. As such, it is only through my creative force that you may find happiness, joy, abundance, peace and fulfillment. I am the only force within you that can deliver true fulfillment and love. Any belief otherwise shall bring chaos and eventual destruction.*

***Build me, feed me and let me be your devoted companion for all of your days.*** *Take hold of me and I will show you that the impossible may be accomplished, that all blockades will be swept away, and any giants in your path will be cast aside as ants.*

*Go about your life and hold the ideals you so desire in your mind! Do not relinquish control of them, until such ideals are reality. Everything you seek will be delivered to you, but you must stand firm.*

*Do not give your attention to thoughts of fear, lack, resentment and failure. Accept only love and freely give.* ***Then enthrone in your mind the deepest desires of your heart!*** *Only hold on to ideals and beliefs that serve to strengthen our connection, for I will not let you down. I will not fail you!*

*I am the same creative force which shaped this Universe, molded the mountains, forged canyons and set all life into motion! I am all things; I am God Force, the First Cause. If you align yourself with me, then all is possible. A path will be made where none did exist! Abundance shall arise where there was once poverty! Courage will prevail while others cower in fear! Strength will come forward when others are frail like glass! Direction will be found amidst chaos!*

*Take heed of this point and commit it to memory:* **The world belongs to me; therefore, it belongs to one who allows me to serve them!**

*This is the truth of any man or woman who has attained success, peace and fulfillment in life. Forgive yourself and then forgive anyone who has hurt you along your path. Nothing is wasted as all is experience. All circumstance no matter how bleak is preparation for the greater good that awaits you.* **Release the fallacy of loss and then take hold of my power!**

*People will be in awe at your ability, and gaze in amazement at the miraculous life you have created. You will know that, with your invisible ally at your side, you can never fail. You could never fail!*

It is no accident that these words have impacted you in a reassuring and empowering manner. It is no coincidence if you feel powerful and strong at this moment, as you are, once again, connected to your creative self, to your true self. The power you feel is because of your connection to this self, and because of an understanding of **your greatest truth.** Hang on to this power. Hold fast to your truth, and *do not let your deepest desire go!* Embrace it at all times, no matter how dark the hour or how bleak the situation. The meager storm shall always pass; together we are always greater!

Apply this truth, because it is your birthright, your narrative and your absolute essence. If you forget it or become wayward, re-read and re-trace my journey. You will remember it and come once again to the place you are now. You shall re-experience the connection you now feel. It is then, that you may begin again.

Remain connected to this power, *as this is the person you were created to be and this is how you were designed to operate!* Continue to foster your creative self, and others will marvel at your ease and power over the world around you. They shall wonder how you became so triumphant, so strong, yet, so delightful.

Share this story and its wisdom, and then watch as others are drawn with fascination and amazement to the magical phenomenon that is YOU!

*F*aithfully yours,

William S. Boyle
February 1949

## Visit Us Online Today!

WWW.YOURGREATESTTRUTH.COM
WWW.YOURULTIMATEWEALTH.COM

**Your Greatest Truth**

A Journey Uncovering
The Great Secret of Life

They will wonder how you
became so successful, so giving

...and so happy

Your Greatest Truth

DARIUS M. BARAZANDEH, ESQUIRE

## More for You!

- Free Audio Downloads!
- Live Event Information! -Coming Near You!
- Continued Learning and NEW Releases!
- World-Wide Discussion of 'Your Greatest Truth' Book!
- Uncovering Your 'Overwhelming Desire' and Your True Power!

I am so excited to share many more exciting lessons and teachings with each of you! I have assembled information to make the greatness that you feel now a part of your life always!

The journey continues and I look forward to meeting each of you! You may contact us at: taxen terp ris es@yah oo.com or by calling 713 961 1134.

Darius and Tricia Barazandeh